A. W. W

Selections From the Letters of
Thomas Sergeant Perry

THE MACMILLAN COMPANY
NEW YORK . BOSTON . CHICAGO . DALLAS
ATLANTA . SAN FRANCISCO

MACMILLAN & CO., Limited
LONDON . BOMBAY . CALCUTTA
MELBOURNE

THE MACMILLAN COMPANY
OF CANADA, Limited
TORONTO

THOMAS SERGEANT PERRY

Selections From the Letters of
Thomas Sergeant Perry

EDITED, WITH AN INTRODUCTION, BY
EDWIN ARLINGTON ROBINSON

NEW YORK
THE MACMILLAN COMPANY
1929

COPYRIGHT, 1929,
BY THE MACMILLAN COMPANY.

All rights reserved, including the right of reproduction
in whole or in part in any form.

Set up and printed.
Published October, 1929.

SET UP BY BROWN BROTHERS LINOTYPERS
PRINTED IN THE UNITED STATES OF AMERICA
BY THE CORNWALL PRESS

CONTENTS

	PAGE
INTRODUCTION	1
BIOGRAPHICAL NOTE	15
TO MRS. JOHN LA FARGE	17
TO MRS. CHRISTOPHER GRANT PERRY	20
TO MOORFIELD STOREY	28
TO WILLIAM JAMES	39
TO THE REVD. H. W. FAY	52
TO JOHN T. MORSE, JR.	61
TO SALOMON REINACH	176
TO JOSEPH C. GREW	222
APPENDIX	251

INTRODUCTION

ANYONE who had the privilege of knowing personally the subject of this volume will be glad to find him again in these few letters of his which have been selected from the many hundreds that he wrote; and those who did not know him will find in them at least a reflection of a personality that was as engaging as it was unusual, as facetious as it was ferocious, and as amiable as it was annihilating. He was not always engaging or facetious or amiable, but even in his depressions and indignations he was always distinguished. After the surrender of Cervera at Santiago, an American officer is reported to have said, "It is asking a great deal of any man to climb aboard an enemy's battleship with nothing but his sword and his underclothes to distinguish him, and still look like an admiral, but Cervera did it." Thomas Sergeant Perry could have done it, if he had been an admiral—or, like his illustrious ancestor, a commodore.

But with all his dignity and intelligence, and with all his youthful activity as a boatman and a swimmer, one doubts if he would have been a happy admiral, or commodore, or if in later life he would have been altogether at ease or at home on the ocean. He must have admired the ocean, as he admired all sublime

Introduction

and magnificent things, and he had been over it to a considerable extent; yet one suspects that, like Lucretius, he found it on the whole more attractive and more impressive when studied comfortably from the shore. On land he was an indomitable walker and tennis-player and bicycle-rider, and yet he was not, in any proper way of speaking, a man of action. He was a man of books. He liked physical exercise, and always took good care of the remarkable body with which he was born, and with which, fortunately, he never had much trouble until old age came upon him, rather swiftly and kindly, and with far less pain than is usually allotted for mortals before their release. But he was born a man of books, and a man of books he lived and died.

He was a great reader, a great friend, and a great gentleman. Whether or not he might have been a great writer is more than one can say, for he never took the trouble to find out. He was an accomplished writer always, or when he chose to be one, and perhaps he was content to let it go at that. He left mostly to others the pangs and pleasures of literary creation, holding himself always in readiness to enjoy or to execrate the result. Alone in his study, with a troublesome world forgotten and out of his way, he made one think sometimes of an experienced and insatiable spider—beneficent or terrible, as the case might be—waiting there to suck the living juice, if he found it, of anything literary that might fly into his clutches. A taste, and often a glance, was enough

Introduction

to tell him the quality of his prey. A native sophistication, long disciplined, served as a protection against the ephemeral and the unsubstantial. For one who read so much, and along so many lines, he lost an incredibly small amount of time in experimenting with mistakes or in getting himself involved in voluminous and able works that might command his respect without arousing his interest. Once in a while, however, he would read such a work, and he would sigh with a scholar's recognition of so much toil and learning gone to the making of so little that was alive. Such books were monuments, perhaps, but to him it was almost a personal sorrow that a writer should be at the same time so competent and so hard to read. But they were books, all the same; they were worthy and admirable books, and were not to be dismissed with levity or with disrespect. They were like some worthy and admirable people whom he would rather not have in the house.

There is no careless exaggeration in saying that books to him were like people. Books to him were living things, and a world without them would have been, in his estimation, as complete an inferno as the most diabolical of medieval minds could have imagined for the damnedest of heretics. Books were the next thing to the breath of life to him, and without them the breath of life itself would have been, so far as he was concerned, a phenomenon hardly worthy of investigation, and surely not one to be prolonged. He regarded life frankly, and without com-

Introduction

plaint or criticism, as a mystery so tragic and bewildering as to be beyond all human comprehension or conjecture, and had therefore not much veneration for metaphysical philosophers. "Philosophy," he said one day, with all possible cheerfulness, "is at its best and highest the attempt of someone to tell me what he doesn't know." He always respected, on the other hand, the religious convictions of his friends, though it would be a false loyalty to pretend that he gave much thought to them, or that he attached to them any particular significance beyond the comfort that others might find in them. In the meantime he estimated character and conduct far beyond accomplishment or glory, and acknowledged only with sorrow and reluctance that a great genius was not always a great man. Sometimes, again, his prejudices, which were active and incurable, may have blinded or deafened him to the enjoyment of beauty that he would not see or hear. He had, for example, so violent a dislike for Wagner as a man that he would listen to his music only under compulsion. He would gladly have found pretty much the same tom-cats and valerian in parts of the *Ring* and in *Tristan* that the late Dr. Max Nordau succeeded once in finding there. But his prejudices, though violent and expensive, as prejudices are likely to be, were for the most part harmless, and were perhaps more picturesque than important. His really righteous indignations came from the depths of his sincerity and his experience.

[4]

Introduction

Although an aristocrat by birth and instinct and environment, he was far more democratic in his feelings and interests than were most of the professional proletarians who might have regarded him as one of the last of the Boston Brahmins, or as an exclusive conservative clinging sadly to the crumbling remnants of the old order. But he was too energetic and too sensible for that. He knew, like many others, that the Great War had carried away with it the world that he had known, and in which he had best belonged; he knew also that time was at his heels, and that the new world would somehow take care of itself without him. He was undoubtedly more at home with his Victorian memories than with his twentieth century questionings and apprehensions—which occupied but a small part of his time. The new order, or disorder, might destroy the landscape, along with other familiar things that he had liked, but it could not destroy his books—a dispensation for which he was snugly thankful. It could even produce new books that he could read and enjoy. Though nurtured on the classics, and still on easy terms with his Latin and Greek, he surprised himself and all his friends in his later years by learning Russian—not the alphabet and how-do-you-do, but the whole formidable language—and in reading almost everything in Russian that could be called literature. His naturally realistic, or rationalistic, mind found at last in the plays and tales of Chekov something for which he had been always looking, and he admired them

Introduction

beyond measure for their competence and honesty, and for their avoidance of any attempt to blur man's finite vision with misty glimmerings of the infinite. When I told him once that it was this very quality in Chekov that kept him from being really great, he agreed with me, rather to my surprise, and continued, naturally and rightly, in his praise of *The Three Sisters*.

If I have called him—by implication, at least—a Victorian, I have done so with a complete conviction that he would have no sort of objection. For that, with his temperament and his intellectual heritage, he could not very well have been anything else. He flayed America, but he remained always an American at heart. He loved England, and the English tradition, but he had little patience with anything that savored of Anglomania—as he revealed one day to an earnest medievalist who deplored the encroachments of time and change, and especially the formation of republics. "Perry," he said, "there are times when I yearn to be a subject."—"What's the matter?" said Perry. "Aren't you contented with being an object?"—He was not often so abrupt or so incisive as that. He may have eaten something that he should not have eaten, or he may have had a twinge of gout. With a sense of humor that was always comprehensive, he would say that his ancestors had all the fun, leaving for him a few fingers that should have been theirs. Fortunately it was only an occasional visitor, and did not interfere with his reading of Chekov, or

Introduction

with his pleasure in not having to read *Salammbô*—against which remarkable production he maintained an animosity that was as respectful as it was unalterable. "It must be a masterpiece," he would say, "for people say so who should know. There's nothing wrong with it, except that it isn't to be read." And so the matter was settled for ever. He did not have to read a book in order to know that it was not written for him; and his literary prejudices at least, must have robbed him of far less than they spared. He was a life-long friend of Henry James, admiring him both as a writer and as a man; but he found too many words in the later novels, and simply would not read them, even for love; and there would have been no especial sense in his reading them, for he could not possibly have enjoyed them. By that time James had invented a new language, which his old friend had never found time to learn. Perhaps Russian had been enough.

Having read almost everything when he was young, he found difficulty, as he approached old age, in reading any fiction that was not Russian. Novels, generally speaking, were pretty well behind him now, although he read nearly every other sort of book imaginable—excepting philosophy, which he had always eyed askance. Novels mostly wearied him. "If they are true to life," he would say, "they are only depressing. If they are not true to life, they are only silly; and novels are too long anyhow." Granting the general validity of all that, one may still be haunted

Introduction

by a few lingering uncertainties; for while *Madame Bovary* and *The Mayor of Casterbridge* were too long, five volumes of the Letters of X. Doudon, which had a special place of honor in his library, were not long enough; and Professor Moore's two mighty volumes on *Judaism* were apparently just right—as no doubt they are. At any rate, he caressed them with approving hands, and praised them, with no reference to their length, in a way that would surely have been a joy to their learned author, had he been there.

But it must not be inferred from the foregoing remarks that he was always solemn in his later years, for he could approve almost anything that was in its way first rate. He could relish an occasional dash of vulgarity, if it was not cheap, and he could enjoy thoroughly any amount of nonsense that was good nonsense. Always apart from a few prejudices—which on the whole made him only the more human and interesting—his *flair* for the best was all but infallible. He was fastidious, but he was far from being antiquated or ungenerous in his likes and dislikes. Though he clung fondly to the past, he was watchful all the time of what the younger men were doing, here and abroad; and as I have no personal acquaintance with Mr. T. S. Eliot or Mr. Van Wyck Brooks, it will do no harm for me to mention here his lively and especial interest in their work. By way of antithesis, it may also be interesting to know that he got a great deal of satisfaction from the racy vigor

Introduction

of the late William Marion Reedy, and often wished that the best of his editorials might be made available in a book—an enterprise, by the way, that is still possible.

With all his courtesy, his cheerfulness, and his charm, he was, I suppose, in our careless and rather meaningless use of the word, a pessimist. Whatever he was, he was not an optimist. He accepted gracefully his condition as a member of the human race, although he never quite succeeded in discovering any satisfactory reason why such a race should have been called into existence. On the other hand, he was in no sense an atheist. He would have considered atheism ridiculous, if only for its assumption of a knowledge that no human being could possibly possess. Not having inherited or acquired a special interest in the abstract or the mystical, he simply left such questions to others who valued them, thus quietly avoiding what would have been for him a futile controversy over the unknowable. He liked best the things that he could see and feel and get hold of. The substance of things hoped for and the evidence of things not seen may have comforted him somewhat as a rare morsel of intellectual humor, but it could never have sustained him on a long and patient journey through one life to another. He found enough in this life that was mysterious and bewildering, and saw no good reason for exploring or disturbing eternity for an evidence of new uncertainties. He was an incurious agnostic. At the same time he was

Introduction

one of the best and cleanest men that ever lived. Dirt, whether physical or mental, was simply dirt to him, and it was nothing more—except when transmuted by the admixture of an impudent and irresistible genius. He would never have tolerated, for example, any improvement of Rabelais or of Aristophanes, or any of the authentic giants. Greatness might have its own way, but littleness had best be careful. His few attempts to read some of the "dirty little people," as he called them, of to-day, were brief and painful, and his pity for their misguided effort was profound.

For that matter, his sorrow for mankind, and especially for womankind, was also profound, although he never said much about it. His reticences were as incurable as cloudy weather while they lasted, and were quite as misleading. Strangers might readily have supposed that he was "always like that", and so might have been ridiculously mistaken—not to say unfortunate. "Charm" is a word not often applied to men so masculine as he, yet he had it to a degree that might have been, and probably was, sometimes, the despair of women. When he was in the mood, or when he took the trouble, he could make his conversation an art in which he was likely to be challenged by few competitors. When he was not in the mood, he said nothing, or nothing remarkable; and one was left to wonder what was going on in his mind—which, though crotchety sometimes, was surely seldom idle.

There were sorrows in his life, and there must have

Introduction

been the disappointments that are so much of life; and there was one injustice that left a permanent mark upon him. But his native courtesy and poise covered all his pains and his problems pretty thoroughly from the knowledge of other people—though not always. Not always, of course; for then he would not have been human—and he was eminently human. During his later years—which were clouded by a long bereavement to which he seldom referred, and for which nothing more could be done—my talk with him turned one day to the arts in general, and to the heavy penalty so many times exacted by fate for their production. During this talk I happened to mention Tasso in prison, without the manuscript of his great poem, with no knowledge of where it might be, and with no certain knowledge that it was even in existence. At that a complete change came over him. He looked at me with a sort of cold fire in his eyes, and his body and his voice trembled as he spoke: "That simply goes to show," he said, pointing a forefinger at me, "that there is absolutely no limit to what the human heart can endure." A few minutes later he was as cheerful and as genial as ever, and was praising Chekov with possibly a little more than his usual enthusiasm.

He always insisted that he was not a writer, which was a fairly obvious nonsense. If he meant that he was not a great creator—a great poet, a great novelist, or a great what-not—he was probably right; yet if his impulse had been only a little stronger, he might

Introduction

easily have written volumes of brilliant and authoritative criticism, or of almost anything that would have given his intellect and his personality a free range. But there was one insuperable obstacle in the way, and one that he appears never to have striven seriously to overcome. So much writing as all that, and the time necessarily involved, would have interfered seriously with his reading. There were books enough without his, he may have reasoned; and some of them, even some of those by the younger men, were not so bad. And there was always the inexhaustible past.

Considering him in retrospect, and as he was born to be, I see him rather as one of the great appreciators—without whom there would be no great writers, or artists of any sort—than as a dynamic and predestined penman. He enjoyed writing letters, but it is difficult to believe that he really enjoyed the writing of books. If he had enjoyed writing them, he would have written more of them—having every conceivable opportunity. His literary ambitions may never have worried or excited him half so much as they worried and excited his friends. It would not be fantastic or extravagant to believe that the one thing he really cared about and wanted, apart from his family, his friends, and his books, was denied him by a twist of fate that partly concealed itself in the manifold ramifications of academic diplomacy. He would have given the best of himself to younger men with more joy and satisfaction than he would ever

Introduction

have had from the applause of his contemporaries. He might have welcomed fame, if he had found it waiting for him at his door, but he would never have been deceived by it, and would never have gone far from his books and his friends for the sake of its unreliable acquaintance. He must have been conscious of much to give that was not to be given, yet here again he never criticised or complained. Whatever his thoughts or feelings or opinions may have been, he kept them to himself. He was a great gentleman, and a great friend; and his personality was one that was remembered wherever he went, and long after the man himself had vanished. He was not the less valuable and rare for not having had the dictation of his destiny, or for not having made a loud noise with his name.

In the foregoing paragraphs, which are as sincere as they are inadequate, it will be seen that nothing of a biographical nature has been attempted. For an admirable account of his life, the reader is referred to *Thomas Sergeant Perry: A Memoir* (Boston, 1929) by his old friend John T. Morse, Jr. The following letters and selections, which call for little or no editorial illumination, will be found remarkably easy to read—although they are no better, perhaps, than many others that might have been selected.

In acknowledging gratefully my indebtedness to Mrs. Perry and to Miss Margaret Perry for their invaluable assistance in the preparation of this vol-

Introduction

ume, I can only hope that the result may not be too far from what they wished it to be. The letters themselves, I trust, will ensure the evasion of any violent disapproval.

E. A. R.

New York, January 21, 1929.

BIOGRAPHICAL NOTE

Thomas Sergeant Perry was born at Newport, Rhode Island, January 23, 1845, the third child of Christopher Grant and Frances (Sergeant) Perry. Commodore Oliver Hazard Perry of Lake Erie fame was his grandfather, and Commodore Matthew Calbraith Perry, noted for his negotiations with Japan, was his great-uncle. Benjamin Franklin, on his mother's side, was his great-great-grandfather. After his graduation from Harvard in 1866 he went abroad for further study, and on his return he was for a time tutor in French and German at Harvard, a position which he resigned to become editor of the "North American Review." After this he was instructor in English at Harvard for five years. On April 9, 1874, he married Miss Lilla Cabot, the daughter of Dr. Samuel Cabot, of Boston. He lived abroad for several years with his family, and in 1897 accepted an invitation to Japan, where for three years he was Professor of English Literature at the Keiogijiku University. On his return to this country he resumed his residence in Boston, having also a summer place in Hancock, New Hampshire. He died at 312 Marlborough Street, his Boston house, on May 7, 1928.

Among his published writings, not including many

Biographical Note

translations and critical articles, are the following books: "Life and Letters of Francis Lieber," 1882; "English Literature in the Eighteenth Century," 1883; "From Opitz to Lessing," 1885; "The Evolution of the Snob," 1887; "History of Greek Literature," 1890; "John Fiske," 1906.

I

(*To Mrs. John La Farge* [1])

[To Miss Emily La Farge, on receiving the news of her birth]

Cambridge, Sunday, Nov. 8, 1863. My dear m (Little Em'(ily)). Your advent has cast a thrill of joy over my existence, and more especially as I hear that yr. resemblance to yr. mother in mind, manners, and person is truly remarkable. I can congratulate her without difficulty, but I am afraid that yr. previous obscurity was better for you than the precarious enjoyment of this transitory existence. Now if there is anything on wh. I particularly pride myself, it is on my intimate knowledge of the workings of the female heart: therefore listen to T. S. P. But no, I will not here blight yr. tender infancy when all is smiling around you with an account of the hollowness of all things and how dolls (what do you, *now,* know of dolls?) are filled with sawdust. But think of yr. beginning to write and beginning to spell! Do you not shudder in yr. cradle? The crude ideas you will form, how you will believe me a giant, and one to be very firmly (excuse the adjective, I might better have said, thoroughly) respected;

[1] Mr. Perry's elder sister.

Thomas Sergeant Perry

T. S. P. being respected!!! (Those marks after respected are indicative (also, as you will soon know the name of a mood) of astonishment). With what exquisite enjoyment you will play dolls with 'Liza blank! The most oriental imagination fails in trying to portray the dolls your generation will play with. Well do I recollect the hickory nut heads of mamma's dolls, with huge books for housewalls.

But there is a darker side yet. Yr. brother, Grant, will cruelly bully you. Days of wretchedness, when agony is well-nigh crushing you, when you will contemplate suicide, because you can't go to so and so's party. The heart-rending at not being allowed to go down to dinner. The anguish (I shudder as I write it), the anguish at being sent off to bed before you're sleepy. But why do I poison yr. life thus early? You had better learn them by yourself, some might say. But I deny it, fly with me, to some desert isle, there I will observe and nurture yr. slumbering intelligence, there, free fm. prejudice and pomp we will live. Come now while it is yet time, flee, have I not a "hand"? Let us first subscribe to the *London Illustrated News* and the *Cornhill Magazine,* and what more do we need? Conceal this fm. everyone. I rely on yr. discretion. Remember me kindly to yr. mother and father and
   Believe me always
         Yr. affectionate Uncle
              T. S. Perry, '66.

To Mrs. John La Farge

Hancock, N. H., Oct. 12, 1922. Dear Mardj:
Many thinks for your note and the really pretty medal. I am horrified by the tale of burglary, and next door! Those gentlemen are very formal and like to take houses in order, so beware! I think you had better send all your most valuable possessions to me at once, beginning with those silver candlesticks. I will look upon them as my own and guard them well. With the sword of Com. Perry I am invincible, and *no one* shall get them from me.

II

(To Mrs. Christopher Grant Perry)

Tokyo, May 20, 1898. . . . The garden party took place last Monday, and I met Marquis Ito, the prime minister, and a lot of lesser nobles whose names and titles would fill three sheets. It was amusing that I, naturally of a modest disposition, should be thus made prominent. I was as polite as I know how to be and said everything agreeable that I could think of, and, as I told Lilla, my position was as if I should go to England as the grandnephew of Wm. the Conqueror. B. Franklin[1] is nowhere! I had throughout the entertainment a feeling that my clothes were very neat. I had sat with my legs out straight before me, not to crinkle my trousers, for at least half an hour. My hat, tho' 4 yrs. old, was by universal consent the newest there. (A friend of mine has told me that he was at a party in Japan, and saw a native of the country in a dress-suit. Everything was complete except that he had forgotten, or neglected, to put on a shirt of any kind.) I was introduced to about 200 noblemen and gentry, and I had a lot of cards given me by people who seem to me to have taken their names from tea-chests. I am

[1] Benjamin Franklin was Mr. Perry's great-great-grandfather.

To Mrs. Christopher Grant Perry

unaccustomed to such incense. I am not used to meeting prime ministers, and my heart smiled within me while all this circus was going on. The fact that I was tall also helped to carry me thro' the ceremonies. . . .

Tokyo: Feb. 16, 1899. . . . Yesterday L.[1] and I went to see a curious ceremony, that of dedicating to one of the eight million Shinto deities, a new sword. Offerings were made to the gods, with the accompaniment of music not to be distinguished from catcalls. Prayers were offered by a priest and we all laid little branches tied in white paper before the shrine. L. is the first woman who has ever seen the rites, from which women are always excluded. They are a curious race and pagan down to the ground.

Tokyo: April 13. . . . Far be it from me to raise my voice in howls, but I can't help wondering how you all are. . . . Last evening we went to a great ball at Marquis Nabeshima's, where was an Imperial Highness to whom I was presented. Which particular prince it was I don't know, but he stood about 4½ ft. high and chatted with interest about the late, the later, Commodore Perry. There was the most gorgeous crowd of uniforms there, English, German, Russian; the Chinese legation patiently strolled about in the anterooms: it was all very amusing. The house

---

[1] Throughout these letters, "L." is for Mrs. Perry, "M.," "E.," and "A." for his daughters Margaret, Edith and Alice.

is a gorgeous one and it was all very fine, except the champagne, which wasn't fit to drink—That is one of the weak points of Japanese civilization, that they cannot distinguish between the real and the imitation wine of this brand. Everything else was most tempting. . . . Mrs. Chas. Homans is here, a friend of ours from Boston. She came just too late for the firewalking. Some one wired to her: "Firewalking Sunday. Come." The despatch read: "Fine walking Sunday. Come." Since she had no special yearning for a promenade after church, she did not hasten her steps and missed it. Col. Churchill told me last night that the whole point of the miracle consists in getting a lot of salt on your feet, and the other morning when the policeman kindly called to tell us our chimney was on fire, we proved to his satisfaction, and our own, how good salt was on such occasions, as well as in miracles. The Japs hardly use it at all, outside of miracles, not even in soup. . . .

Tokyo: May 10. . . . I wrote to you a few days ago that L. and E. had been to Miyanoshita. On leaving L. wished to distribute some largess to the most amiable and obliging servants, and for that purpose gave what she at the time thought to be one yen, but afterwards conjectured to be a five-yen note. Yesterday we rec'd a letter of which this is a copy:

To Mrs. Christopher Grant Perry

To Miss etc.
Madam,
As there were unfortunately a great many visitors in my place during your staying I am very sorry that I could not pay you any attention. Notwithstanding to the careless treatment you gave a waitress five yen note at the time of your departure but I know their attendance was not worthy to be presented so many money, on the contrary it is enough, to be given one yen so that I return you the ballance (4 yen) by the postal many order. Please regard our compliments to your all families.
Yours truly, etc.

What do you think of that? . . .

. . . Today two globe-trotting young American girls tiffined here. One of them said, speaking of European-Japanese marriages, that she couldn't understand them, that she felt about them as she supposed English people felt about marriages with Americans. I said I had not observed any hesitation about these, that rather, so far as I had noticed, they had been the cause of complaint on both sides of the Atlantic. She explained that she meant the objection Englishwomen felt to marrying American men. I said the feeling must be indeed very intense if it stood in the way of an Englishwoman marrying anyone. Then I went to see her papa and mamma, who (at least, the father) gave me less disgust. . . .

Tokyo: May 27. . . . Tomorrow I have to go to a banquet of students and graduates of the Keio at a

Japanese restaurant. I had hoped that it might be possible for me to arrange in such a way that I could eat an early dinner before I went, for a Japanese dinner is the most elusive joy possible. In the first place, one has to take off one's shoes and paddle about in stockings; then what food you get you have to eat sitting on the floor with chop-sticks; it is served in courses at most uncertain and tedious intervals, so that you never can tell whether the dinner is over or not, and then the food! It is really not tempting: fish in various forms, that is good; soups, they are often good, messes variously compounded of beans, pomatum and glue—it is a dreadful trial, and I wish I could swallow a Christian dinner first, but I shall have to assume the Yellow Man's burden and pretend that I am enjoying myself.

June 6. The dinner was as I expected. It began only at 7.30 so that I had plenty of time to eat something at home, which would have been better, for as it was I could eat nothing there. They set before me: a bowl of warm water, with a little fish-skin in it and a few scraps of white fish on it which I ate. This mess also contained a globular mass; what it was I know not, but I swallowed it. It tasted like hominy. On another dish was a mass of something that looked like lard, some fish stuff, and two crayfish. These crayfish I ate. On the same platter was a sweet mess, of chestnuts covered, apparently, with applesauce. There was a choice assortment of raw fish. They then

To Mrs. Christopher Grant Perry

brought what looked like cold roast chicken, and my hopes revived; it turned out to be cold boiled fish, and my hopes fell. That was all: no rice, no bread, no salt. I couldn't help thinking what a delightful meal it would have been for a cat, and it was served, as I told you it would be, as one serves a meal for a cat, on the floor. The consequence is that I shall go to my grave with one dinner less than my normal account. It was most unfortunate.

Tokyo: April 21, 1900. . . . If you were here and should see me removing vol. II of Millhouse's Ital. Dictionary and placing it with some difficulty in my high hat, you would wonder what I was doing, whereas this is my usual habit when the day comes for me to go to a garden party. It is necessary on such occasions to wear a top hat and a frock coat, and my hat in seclusion suffers curiously from the Japanese climate, and from an oval shape changes to a circle. In consequence the hat when placed upon the head is most uncomfortable and then totters under even the lightest breeze. Today is cold, gray and windy, so that it will require a good deal of imagination to make this garden-party pleasant. It is given by the Sonodas in honour of Baron Hayashi, newly appointed minister to England, with whom I dined at the Kirkwoods a month or two ago. He leaves in a few days, and is now "eating his way out."

Yesterday there was the Imperial garden-party and tho' the morning had been really warm (over 70°)

Thomas Sergeant Perry

at 12.30 there came up a high cold N.E. wind which soon cooled the air. High hats are of course part of the uniform and it was amusing for those who wore the tighter felt headcovering to watch their more highly decorated brethren clinging to their shiny top-pieces. My hat would make no great impression in New York or Paris, but here it shines like a crown elsewhere, for it is quite new (for Japan) having been bought in 1894, six yrs. ago, and, when carefully brushed, is very effective. Some of the hats would make a scarecrow contemptuous. . . .

Tokyo: Nov. 11. . . . The dinner took place. Everyone came at the moment. . . . It went off very well, tho' cooks in Japan *insist* on serving game and salad before the roast. I storm in vain, and then, hearing that violent words are ineffectual in Japan, I reason, urge, persuade. They smile more sweetly than ever and promise everything, but when dinner is served, there comes the game with salad and after it the roast! I am not the only sufferer, it is the cause of much international unhappiness. The Japs may conquer Peking as often as you will, but they won't be a truly civilized race until they correct this fundamental error. But then, as I said to Mme. Iswolsky (lest, oh, horrors! she should hold me responsible for this awful fault), they begin their own dinners with fruit and finish them with raw oysters. How can these lamentable pagans be expected to comprehend our conventions? . . . Even now it's not too cold. In

To Mrs. Christopher Grant Perry

fact, it's mild. As I have indicated, I prefer mildness. Grant me an equable temperature and I am equally equable. Yet, such is the evil nature of man, of other men, the moment they find a quiet thermometer, they are miserable. Tomorrow there is a ball. Saturday I go to a horrid Jap. dinner, of my students. I have now learned wisdom and, before starting, I shall eat a solid meal. Only that way lies happiness. I shall paddle about in stocking-feet so long as may be and then home early. . . .

III

(To Moorfield Storey)

Newport, July 21, 1864. . . . As to the White Mts. I don't think I can spare from here more than 2 weeks or at the most not more than 3 days more. At least my mother wishes me to return by that time, but it will depend principally upon the supply of green-backs. I suppose that the question of money is also of interest to you and therefore make bold to ask you if you know at all how much would be necessary for 2 weeks. When I went before I took $40.00 with me but at the end of about a week I lost all that was left on top of a mountain and had to come home penniless and humiliated by the charge of not being able to take care of my money. But I suppose hotel-prices like everything else has riz. Therefore I would like to have some idea of the amount necessary. If you have any such knowledge, which I must say is exceedingly improbable, pray set the figure rather above, than below the mean, for there's no knowing what will turn up, and parents who only see their offspring twice a year don't get as disgusted with them as they would if they had to see them every week. . . .

Paris, Dec. 3, 1866. . . . If you and Strat [1] have

---

[1] Charles E. Stratton, of Boston.

To Moorfield Storey

received all my letters I suppose you expect an account of today's lectures, a brief synopsis of some frog-eaten remarks on the varying use of *a, ab, abs* and *absque,* or a full selection from the French Andrew's & Stoddard's grammar, but like me this morning you are doomed to disappointment. I got up early after a sleepless night, feeling as we all did about the 1st of Sept. 1862, and bought a blankbook, a good and thick one for notes on the lectures, and went around the corner at 12 to the Sorbonne, but I found I had been misinformed (probably a bit of hazing) and that none of the courses began either there or at the Collège de France until next week; so I have some more time to lie heavy on my hands, only to be varied by writing letters and by French lessons which begin on Wednesday. . . . But at any rate I expect to learn a good deal of French, and to hear some excellent lectures. The course on Latin Poetry at the Collège (the 2 about the Æneid) is under the direction of Sainte-Beuve, tho' he never lectures himself. Paul Jenet is rather a helion. So is Alf. Maury. Laboulaye, too, is a very popular lecturer and to some of his I shall try to go. Then there is an exhilarating tone of *work* about the place. For a full account of their way of running all this you must wait yet a little. If I don't go to Germany, I shall probably come home in about a year. What I may do is a blank. From what I have written about this winter you will see that it promises to be an instructive one, and were I sitting on a rosebush, having cologne squirted into my eyes by unwashed Ethiopian slaves, in a flea-ridden boat on the Nile, I would be sighing for my present chances of work. . . .

Venice: Apr. 13, 1889. If my congratulations on the birth of Charles Moorfield have been long a-coming they are not on that account less genuine. I often think of him, and if he were only here I should like to begin his education with a hasty sketch of Venetian history, pointing out to him the perils of republics, to carry out the lessons of history through the remoter past and down to the election of Harrison. Then hand in hand we would walk thro' the galleries and I should point out to him the masterpieces of the limner's art, explaining to him, not too dogmatically I hope, the various beauties of Titian, Gian Bellini, Tintoretto, Carpaccio, and Bonifazio; urging him meanwhile to look and think for himself, and listening patiently to whatever suggestions—possibly fraught with some new explanation—he might wish to make.

I know that he would like the churches, and while I would gladly let him gaze his fill at the lights and curtains, and altars and pictures and tombs, yet, without bigotry, I should rather hint than urge the perils of the Church of Rome, and give him a brief sketch of Protestantism and what it has done, with an account of each separate sect, and a brief anecdotical history of the leading divines of Boston and vicinity. Then we would get into a gondola and I would throw him

To Moorfield Storey

overboard—nay! let me not too rudely stir a fond father's heart and recall all sorts of anxieties! Nay, again, but listen! I would cast him into the water only to teach him to swim, an art best learned in infancy. I know that C. Moorfield would enjoy imbibing almost unconsciously a good deal of miscellaneous information, and I would ask you to send him out by Adams's Express, were it not that we leave Venice tomorrow on our way Parisward. Our infamous proprietor, in spite of written and spoken promises, threatens to double our rent, hoping to make his eternal fortune this Exposition year, and we must return to seek new quarters. . . .

We have been now 6 weeks in Italy and have learned several new ways of shivering; we had often heard of Neapolitan ices and we have a chance to see—a sight rarely vouchsafed to mortal man—Neapolitan snows. But these travellers' woes are soon forgotten and don't bear transportation across the seas. All winter my good wife painted, and with success, for she has two pictures in the *Salon,* one a portrait of Edith and another, of me. You will see them when we get home. We expect to return this summer, tho' just when we sail is uncertain.

As to the row about Harvard College I hear and think a good deal. Of course one so far away doesn't get all the facts and conditions, but to my prejudiced eye it seems rather as if the Overseers were something like the wolf in the fable, seeking an excuse for glutting their indignation towards

Thomas Sergeant Perry

a bad man. They attack him for this matter when they are angry with him simply for existing; small blame to them, perhaps, but it's not justice in its best aspect. As to the interference of the Overseers—if you will let me use the word—I regard it as in every way lamentable, as tending to bring down the ideal of education to suit the notions of outsiders who, by the nature of their occupations, cannot fully understand the desirability of greater freedom. The notions of the Overseers are bourgeois and philistine and will certainly lower the higher education which, at the best, has a very meagre hold in Cambridge, and, *me judice,* stands in far greater need of encouragement than of repression. Always the steps forward have come and must come *ab intra,* and often the outside influences are not beneficial, e.g., when G. Ticknor was sat upon 50 yrs. ago and education for 40 yrs. was petrified. In this case, the present row I mean, if the Overseers establish the power of controlling and trimming the processes of education to suit their own ideas, education will receive another blow and a very serious one. College education will drift away into a system for keeping boys harmless for 4 yrs. instead of growing into something essential for men who hope to work, *which is its only hope for thriving,* etc., etc., etc. But I must tire you with my oft-repeated and Cassandrian wail.

. . . I shan't be at all sorry to get back, and I hope next winter to be able to find you at home of many

To Moorfield Storey

a Sabbath morn and to tell you strange tales of adventuresome travel while C. M. listens with wondering eyes. I have seen many people and many lands, but I return with gratitude to a wise Providence that made me an American. These fellows over here have a magnificent past all around them, but what a present! And, apparently, what a future! But of course America has got to be steered, too. We shall, D.v., have great talks. . . .

. . . Tomorrow we go in early morning to Padua, in P.M. to Brescia for night, see it the next day and on to Milan. There a day or two, then thro' Switzerland to Bâle, and so to Paris, where we resume our Burden, beginning with fight with our proprietor who will, I take it, be surprised when we leave. Oh! for an hour of the legal talent lying idle in the Rialto Building—the perfect image of a Venetian palace!—wherewithal to crush the vile Gaul. I don't like Gauls; I like not the English; I love my country best, one and inseparable, foolish but intelligent.[1] . . .

Paris, June 6, 1889. . . . In reference to Harvard College, I will only say that I did not get my information or ideas from J. M. P. [James Mills Peirce], but the first rather from various sources; the second from the pure ether of eternal justice and my own heaven-born intellects. I will, however, refrain from

---

[1] It will be seen that these opinions and preferences were somewhat modified as the writer grew older.

Thomas Sergeant Perry

enforcing my views on your stolidly recalcitrant self, because 1°, I respect you, and 2°, I have nothing to say on a subject already threadbare. . . .

What storms and things you have in America! We had a little earthquake ourselves a few days ago, just a little wobble that was barely perceptible. You will soon be having commencement and a noble band of Overseers await election. Thank heaven I'm not there to vote for them. . . .

How comes on young Charles Moorfield? Bless him! How does it seem to rock the little tyrant? to listen to his imperious call? to walk the deck with him vociferous? They are a bother, children, but they are fun. And how is the bar, Demosthenes? Does justice rule? And how do you enjoy Republican rule? Over here it is a curious thing, while my dear friend and late neighbour, [General] Boulanger, is away. He seems clean forgotten by the fickle French, but who can tell? The autumn elections still await us. The Boston *Herald* is dull; the *Record,* foul; the *Post* heavy; the *Advertiser,* odious, but nevertheless, send me the 1st paper you can lay your hands on.

. . . I wrote you from Venice; we went thence to Padua, Brescia, Milan, and so home, reaching here Apr. 19, when we moved to our new quarters, where we have, *mirabile dictu,* a bathtub!

Giverny: Sept. 21, 1907. . . . I enclose the enclosed enclosure. May I ask you when you occupied

To Moorfield Storey

your mansion in the aristocratic section of Jamaica Plain, and what sort of a mansion in the skies you expect to occupy if you allow such misrepresentations to go uncorrected? Your claim to be an old Jamaica Plain boy—understand I say a *Jamaica Plain boy*—is as empty as your claim to the ping pong championship. I have received your remarks on the subject and if the question were not already settled, judgment having already been given, now some years ago, by a most competent and duly appointed judge, myself, further discussion is purely academic. Have you forgotten how you burst into tears after a long string of failures to return the ball that was sent to you? How vainly you evoked Hachiman,[1] Baal and other false gods, so that I was delighted that good old James Freeman Clarke was not there to hear you? Don't you remember the procession that insisted on escorting me, amid blare of trumpets and beat of drum through the sinuous streets of the Back Bay to my house? Perhaps you were not there as we passed the darkened residence of James Crafts (the only house not one blaze of light on the way) and above all the clangor of the bands and the, by that time, hoarse roar of the multitude I could hear the screams of Mrs. Crafts weeping for her husband's utter failure in the tournament. I have by my side the beautiful memorial given me by grateful citizens, bearing this simple but sufficient inscription: "To the world's champion in Ping Pong, T. S. Perry, his fellow-

[1] The Japanese god of War.

citizens of Hancock and Boston present this tribute of affection and respect."

I shall never forget the simple becoming words of Judge Dewey on that occasion. T. R. sent a letter strongly recommending athletic sports to gentlemen in their declining years. Of course it is painful to a modest man like me to recall these things, but they will recall to you the true story of the event and after all, Moorfield, your remarks when condensed are merely this: is it likely that after gaining the championship I should go abroad? I ask you, I ask the Moorfield I have known for more than 40 yrs., if it is likely that I had any reason to linger in Boston after the championship was definitely settled and the prize awarded? Your long experience before the intelligent juries of our country must have taught the worthlessness of that, I can't call it argument, of that presentation of the subject.

I hope not to have occasion to refer to this unfortunate matter again. It is the first cloud that has shadowed our old friendship. I have overlooked a great deal, the use of my vast fortune as collateral in wild-cat speculation, the neglect to sell my insurance stock just before the San Francisco earthquake, which I should never have pardoned another man, but the treatment of the ping pong championship is hard to overlook. . . .

Hancock, N. H., Sept. 26, 1920. Your sad exposition of the world's woes came to hand last evening

To Moorfield Storey

and I thank you for it. I should feel blue if it were not that there are so many cures for the present state of things, for what is after all the chronic state of things. Why should we lament when Communism, Socialism, Syndicalism, Bolshevism, stand ready to set things right? You see we always want something else to do our work. . . .

I have just heard that Santayana was denied promotion in Harvard Coll. in 1912 or so, because some prominent overseer said he taught atheism! If this is so (and [James Ford] Rhodes tells me) it is a most scandalous thing, for S. is one of the best men they ever had in the college, one of the best teachers, one of the best influences. Look at his *Little Essays,* just out, made up of extracts from his various works, on all sorts of subjects—a delightful book. Of course the charge is preposterous. The college lost a very brilliant man. I am very angry about it.

Hancock, N. H., January 24, 1928. The varied and alluring manifestations of your bounty surprised me last evening as I was sitting bemoaning an ill-spent life. One delicacy after another emerged from the wrapping-paper. The oddest, I think, was the gold-fish marmalade, the prettiest thing I ever saw and not merely good looking. Receive the thanks of a most grateful family who haven't yet half investigated the crowded hamper. It was very good of you to remember the solemn festival.[1] It finds us still in

---
[1] In celebration of T. S. P.'s eighty-third birthday, January 23.

the country but apparently soon to get to town. Once there I shall try to get to see you. We will together groan over the general horror of all things. I notice that our friend Mr. Borah has risen to oppose the huge navy and I wish I had not so thoroughly undermined his influence as I have done by my eloquent orations. That navy business is the most alarming thing yet. It is Germany over again. We seem anxious to take the place she held and with our awful mania for managing others, we are a peril to mankind. What we need is a good thrashing. See how Germany is improved. Recall what an uplifting there was in France after '70-'71. . . .

IV

(To William James)

Philadelphia, Feb. 4, 1865. Honest William: Alas, why are you not here by my side, to rasp my swollen throat, to bathe my fevered brow, to administer the needful aperient, to hand me the gargle, to put on the blister, to prepare the poultice, to set the broken limb, to apply the grateful cautery, to direct the soothing injection, in short, to practice that art in which you so proudly excel, i.e. (pronounced *'that is'*) the art of medicine.[1] I have been racked as to the throat with a most devilish soreness. I took last night after getting to my bed a hot glass of whiskey punch and covered myself heavily with clothes. I passed a wretched night, dreaming all the time that I was about to go in swimming on a frightfully hot day, but could not get into the water. I need a master-hand to cure me. I may get well under these quacks here, but doubt it. This place is a hole. Taine's *History of English Literature* is not to be had in the whole city, nor is there any Morris Morgan tobacco. Since I have been here I have

[1] William James was at this time a student in the Harvard Medical School.

Thomas Sergeant Perry

gone slightly into the gay whirl of society, seen several hundred young ladies, been skating with them. Have read French novels, one *Le Pays Latin* by H. Murger, which is much poorer than the *Vie de Bohème,* Feydeau's *Fanny,* a most execrably worthless thing, one of Paul de Kock's, moral, but very uninteresting, a little book which at the beginning said that it was going to prove the world had been made in six days, and at the end that it had been proved, though where, I could not find out. Brimley's Essays, weak. Some of Hume's Essays, which are very good indeed. My uncle has given me them in four large volumes. Am to decide of future profession this vacation. Please send me copy of "Investigator" that I may see if place of lecturer against the existence of God is still open. It might not be a bad beginning. Think of Divinity? Damn Divinity and Divines. Of Law? Too big a fool. Of Medicine? Don't know. Jno. Curtis is coming next week. He is an amiable fellow. By the way, do you know how much Seltzer Aperient is needed to have some effect? I have taken several table-spoonsful since dinner, but without result. Adieu, ask brother Harry to write. If James T. Fields, acting by the advice of C. E. Norton, gives him so much per sheet for everything he writes, let not that restrain him. I will pay him an equal sum if he will only write to me. I saw *Enoch Arden* the other night. Good, better than most farces. . . . P. S. Excuse the melancholy which obtains in connection with this

[40]

To William James

letter. You, a doctor, can well understand it, knowing that I'm sick.

Readville, Mass., August 19, 1902. My dear W. J. I received your book [1] in due season. I read it and then I read it again. This I have repeated since. I think it a very important book. The subject is one of which I am absolutely ignorant, so that I cannot judge of it from the inside, so to speak. What I especially admire in it is its unacademic quality, its bringing in human evidence of all sorts from everywhere, whereas—as you will know and say—the desire of everything that seems to be established is to establish itself more firmly, to petrify itself, and to dull innovation. All good work is done in leading people on, instead of urging them to be content with what has been done. You take in testimony from the gutters; the more rigid will disapprove.—The real comment on your book would require a volume and, I daresay, volumes will be hurled at you. At any rate, you have lugged the poor dull human mind a good bit out of the mud, and you have done excellent work. . . . As I said, your book enlarges the field of investigation and gives a *locus standi* to many interesting things. It must have stirred strangely some of your audience.

June 28, 1903. Dear W. J. My felicitations, not merely for the new letters that you may append to

[1] *Varieties of Religious Experience.*

Thomas Sergeant Perry

your already honoured name, but for your too few words at the dinner the other day, in which you created a sensation by uttering the startling paradox that possibly a university concerned itself with matters of thought. They were words of undoubted truth and most well worth saying. The club (social and athletic) side of Cambridge life is so ludicrously prominent that the mere reminder of anything else disturbs the normal movement. I didn't hear you because I abstain from the noisy joys of Commencement as a pious Jew from high mass, but I enjoyed reading the report of the speech in last night's "Transcript." You deserve the gratitude of the Republic. . . .

Paris, March 14, 1905. Dear W. J. Many thanks for your good long letter which was full of interest. A week or so ago I saw Piddington who was passing through Paris on his way to the South, and we had some talk. He seemed to have a very clear notion of what he wanted to do, and of the nature of the problem that lay before him in America. I think he is a clever, practical man who will straighten things out. I was able to give him no new ideas; he is already admirably prepared.—He has taken Hyslop's measure and will, I think, put that gentleman out of the way, but perhaps I am too sanguine. I know I am sanguinary. . . . Yes, Richard Hodgson's death was lamentably premature—to our eyes—he would have written other books, but books seldom convince

To William James

anyone. They buttress the convictions already formed. Still, I don't mean to imply that he would have done no further good work. That I do not think at all. He ought to be able to do good work from the other side, for he knows our difficulties. I am sorry you are not coming here next winter when we expect to be here. I suppose we shall then go home, though after all why I should not spend my declining years in a congenial atmosphere I don't see, and Paris is in many ways very congenial. —The struggle between Church and State interests me mightily. When the other day the Chamber turned out Rouvier, I was furious at their selecting that moment. There has gone in a radical ministry who, it seems to me, are sure to make votes for the Right. But it's not my business.—When you want an interesting book, take Gustave LeBon's *Psychologie de l'Education*. Make them buy it, as also S. Reinach's *Cultes, Mythes et Religions*, 2 vols., Leroux. It's about the most important of new books. I see your works translated, on every stand. . . .

Hancock, N. H., Aug. 21, 1905. I believe you have some part of the responsibility for my writing a Beacon biography of John Fiske. It was a singular choice, for I know nothing of philosophy, of history, of religion, but at any rate the book is done. The publisher says it's too short and loudly cries for more words. It's a strange complaint that a book is too short, certainly a rare one. I can't think excessive brevity is its only fault, and I hope that when you see it you will pardon all its shortcomings.—How comes on your system of philosophy? Have you made mincemeat of all your predecessors? Beware! I hear choppers sharpening to make mincemeat of you. Young R. Pumpelly has succumbed to your eloquence and bursts forth with philosophic raving; his condition is most pitiable and you are responsible. I must write a counterblast against philosophy. It will have one good effect: it will unite you all in common execration of the philistine: monists, dualists, pluralists, etc. I don't even know your nicknames. *My philosophy remains Nietzsche, because when I read him I understand what my contemporaries mean by being imperial and bullying and haters of a brown or black skin. I have no respect for N. (he is a philosopher, and so debarred), but through his pipe blow all the airs of the present.* . . .

Paris, Jan. 22, 1907. I am sending you a *Débats* containing an article by Bourdeau which says what I have always said about philosophy. The wise Italian at length pricks the bubble and I have sent for his book to have one authority in support of my disbelief.—But then, it is your only consolation, he speaks in favour of dogmatism—I mean pragmatism —in which you have been revelling, and he tells me what I suppose you for the moment believe, that here at last is something sound. We shall see.—If I had stayed in Boston, I might have known what prag-

To William James

matism, what real philosophy is; now I can only wait for real proofs. Meanwhile I shall rest satisfied with his destruction and criticism. When Bourdeau carries out his high-sounding threat, I mean to send you his article. He is always most interesting, even to a philistine like me. . . . In November I had a most delightful visit at Rye. Harry [James] and I had many long talks that did my heart good. It was a great pleasure to see him and I am looking forward to his arrival here next month. . . . This Church and State business is most interesting. It is curious how many good Catholics approve the measure.

Paris, March 20, 1907. I have received your glowing circular about pragmatism; it is full of promise about what that great innovation really isn't, but I want to know what it is. This I shall doubtless learn in succeeding *Abdrücke;* with seven lectures before you, you were not going to say all you had to say in the first lesson. What I read filled me with many emotions, what are called "conflicting" emotions. I wanted to go out and bang you, and these symptoms became so violent that nothing would stop them but the thought that I must be a philosopher myself, and so unable to endure any other man's system. This reflection cooled me.—What I really think is that philosophers are what in old times, when the Bible was coming out, used to be called prophets. In prophecy, the prophets were most incompetent; they never got anything right, but they made delicious reading. So do you, and what adds to the reader's delight is your constant whack at anyone else who philosophizes.—I find myself admirably portrayed in your brief sketch of the hard-headed pessimist, hungry for fact. I read over your account of him and me as I look at one of my photographs.—Seriously, I read (past tense) and read (present time) your remarks with delight. They fill me with a desire to become a philosopher myself. I think, now that I am learning the trick, I could do it admirably. Of course, I should go for you, as you go for Ladd and Royce, and as they will go for you in later numbers of the "Popular Science," but I should also go for them. . . .

Giverny par Vernon (Eure), July 11, 1907. I am sending you a *Revue Bleue* with what seems to me a good article in it by Paul Gaultier, a new writer who differs from many by having something to say. —I observe the "Spectator" opens what promises to be a very heavy cannonading on your anarchistic book, and I fancy there will be firing all along the line. The Absolute lives in the lofty (top-lofty) region of Great Thunders. . . .

Paris, Jan. 13, 1909. You can put it to your credit that you have made at least one complete victory; you have made me a reader of philosophy—at least of your philosophy, and there is no other. I have gone so far indeed that I am in danger of starting a theory

To William James

of my own, which is what all philosophers did until your book on Pragmatism appeared. On the whole, I shan't do that; I shall remain a fond, admiring disciple, especially if you feed us such nice fat lumps as the Fechner article in the January "Hibbert". That is what I like, that is the way to look at the world, with large, generous eyes, not blinded by books and repeating what is said in books that merely copy what is in other also copying books. I love that Fechner episode; he sees the world as we see it in all those feelings not in text books, not childish, natural, and perhaps genuine.—Did you ever show me, long ago, anything of Fechner in this sense? What you report of him had to me an air of something I had known. I asked myself if I had read it (when my eyes were blind) under your fostering care, or was it merely a memory of my infancy? It is a noble article. He gives you a magnificent impression (who am I to praise him?) of being an elemental force, of beating poetry and rivalling music in saying those things that can't be said by anyone else. To begin with, he gets away from books—and what a relief that is!—and has all those feelings of suffering in flowers picked, of patience in stone and iron—at least he seems to imply it. If he doesn't, I do. Hitherto philosophy, like learning (and much painting and much music) has been literary, and life is not literary. Even literature is becoming unliterary.—I stop because I am afraid I am simply incoherent. I am overwhelmed with *mauvaise honte,* but you must receive a good many foolish confessions and one more or less can make but little difference. You can throw me into the fire.—I am sending you a most readable letter about the Italian earthquake—you are an amateur of earthquakes—and the last Academy speeches. Yours always, T. S. Perry, homunculus.

Paris, May 5, 1909. I am much obliged to you for your "Pluralistic Universe" which I found awaiting me the other day on my return from a short visit to Berlin. I confess that my education has been so neglected that I can't always follow you. I am too new, too superficial a student of that long abused science to be able to grasp the meaning of new words and phrases, but give me time! I shall get to a fuller understanding, though now I grope in the dark. So long as you go in the house and choke the Absolute, I will stand outside and cheer. Then there are beautiful bits that reward all my patience, such as all on Fechner, the eloquent bit p. 99, etc. I shall read and re-read until I get a firm hold. I am delighted that you, too, found Bergson hard. I read him with delirious joy as if I were going to understand him the next moment, and it was all very fine, but what it was I couldn't say. [Dr. Pierre] Janet greatly admires B. But what can philosophy do except amiably reflect the philosopher's nature? It is an impossible effort to pack the universe into a poor muddled brain. One might as well climb a mountain and try to look round the globe. It is a noble ambition, but a hope-

To William James

less one, and I am glad to see the accursed race (as I once thought them) acknowledging the difficulty....

Paris, May 31, 1909. .... I read your philosophy as the pious read the Good Book. I don't understand much of it, but I am sure it is all true, and that in time I shall get profit from it. The more I read it, the more I begin to see what you are driving at, but I am very stupid. I have a general feeling of gratitude to you for kicking the frozen Absolute and the icy personifications from their perches, though some other fellow will come along, prove you an intruder, and put them all back again. But I shall remain true to the beautiful Fechner, to Bergson (of whom I understand not one word), and to you.—Farewell.

Giverny par Vernon (Eure). Oct. 20, 1909. Dear W. J. I have this morning received your *Truth*. Jesting Pilate is at last answered and I have made up my mind to become an active pragmatist when once I get home. I shall preach the new gospel in the Back Bay. Do you provide a uniform for the saints? Have you devised a grip by means of which we, the elect, may recognize one another?—For my own part, I have never been troubled by any uncertainty as to what is Truth. Truth is what I think. When others think otherwise, they are wrong. But I do wish you would write a book explaining Epistemology. I ran along smoothly until I came across that horrid word, and then I was all at sea. I shall have to look it up

Thomas Sergeant Perry

in the dictionary of philosophical terms before I begin to preach.—What an extraordinary thing philosophy is! And, I egotistically think, that I should at last be caught in its cobweb! It seems to me the anatomy of thought, as dry as a skeleton. But yours is animated with living breath and blood. I love it. —I am putting aside your book to read on shipboard, but I have already made so liberal a provision that I shall read this before I sail, and then it will bear repeated reading before I understand it, especially while I don't know what epistemology is. It reminds me of the first and last sermon I ever listened to, in Trinity Church, Newport, from the inspired lips of the Reverend Darius Brewer. It was on some text like this, "Lord, keep thy servant from presumptuous sins, and let them not have dominion over me" (Psalms). I listened with precocious fervour, thinking I was surely securing eternal bliss, but always embarrassed by the frequent mention of the word presumptuous which conveyed to me no meaning. I have a superficial comprehension of your theories, but when someone in the audience asks me to reconcile him with epistemology, I shall have to feign a nose-bleed.—You have beautifully ennobled philosophy by making it seem human instead of a thing of formulas. Your comparisons and joyous chaff delight me. No wonder the bigwigs hate you. I keep opening your book, reading it with delight. I can never keep it for the ship (I am sure it will bring to shore crew and passengers all devoutly sworn to the new

To William James

faith). I have been reading pp. 57, 58 abt. the general break-up. You are right. So then I most warmly thank you for your kindness in giving me your really delightful book. It is a joy for ever, and when I get home I shall thank you again. My best greetings to all of yours.

V

(To the Revd. H. W. Fay)

Bayreuth: July 26, 1888. . . . The opera (*Parsifal*) began at 4.5. The first act is pretty dull; for the plot of the opera, consult the daily papers. It is foolish enough, Rider Haggard being beaten on his own ground. The singing and acting were very good, and the music faultless, especially in the cunning subdued accompaniment. The scenery is fine. About 6 there was ½ hr.'s intermission, in which I took beer, and we strolled about, seeing Berenson, Arthur Foote, the Dixies, etc., etc., every one, in short, save Mrs. Jack Gardner. The second act was better, the third, after a longer intermission, 7.45-8.30, devoted to more beer and food for which I had to scramble as at a R.R. restaurant, was the finest. Parsifal is got up to look just like Christ; he is baptized by an old hermit, he baptizes a Magdalen who bathes and anoints his feet and indeed anoints them; in short the New Testament is freely drawn on, and the impression is very great. It is never dramatic, but always intensely picturesque and musical. Wagner still seems to me a tremendous charlatan, but very able and impressive in a slow way. . . . One thing is sure, much of his work is *very* dull, but when he is good he

To the Revd. H. W. Fay

is very good. . . . Mrs. Perry and her uncle have gone out to make calls, and this afternoon they see *Meistersinger.* I am quite contented to stay at home, so you see I am not a rabid Wagnerite, tho' it would be as much as my life is worth to say so here. . . . There is humbug in Wagner, and abundant fraudulent admiration, at least among the laity, for his merits.

Dresden: July 28, 1888. We left Bayreuth at 1.35 yesterday P.M. and got here at 9.52. This morning we spent looking at the beautiful pictures in the gallery here; this afternoon Mrs. Perry is devoting to shopping, and I take an idle hour to write to you. She mightily enjoyed the *Meistersinger,* and I cheerfully acknowledge that I know too little of Wagner to appreciate him as he should be appreciated and I know too much about the difficulty of understanding other things to set any value upon my ignorance. He is, I may still say, slow in acts 1 and 2 and great in act 3; he knows how to produce a great final impression. Yesterday morning before leaving Bayreuth we went to the master's grave. I was asked the day before if I didn't want to do this, and I answered, with occult readiness, that it was what I had long wanted to see. (Meaning, my dear Sir, that for many years I had wished to hear of the death of R. Wagner, because I regarded him as a colossal fraud. My esoteric meaning escaped my interlocutor and I explain it thus at length because I find other delicate jokes of mine had escaped even your microscopic eye.) While the *Meistersinger* was raging within, I sat without in the restaurant, on its terrace, gazing at the beauteous view, and talking to the fanatics as they issued from their lair in the entr'actes. Why I was not mobbed in Bayreuth I do not know, unless my immunity is to be ascribed to the refining influence of music, but this delicacy did not extend to the feeding-time in *Parsifal* when horrid scenes of gorging and guzzling "transpired", and the waiters, who, to be sure, hadn't heard a note, cheated in a most masterful manner, and I reclaimed and got 5 marks back from one man who, as it was, I believe got 50 pfennig to the good. . . . By the way, E. Jackson told me today that the young man "with a grandfather," in one of Mark Twain's books, doubtless *A Tramp Abroad,* is a young —— whom I once had under me in Cambridge. . . . I know an amusing story of the way he was sold once in England by some of his playmates who got up among themselves an invitation to Windsor Castle, apparently issuing from Q. Victoria. He was asked out of affection for his grandfather, but, since the Court was in deep mourning, he was requested to dye his red hair black! And he believed it! . . .

Munich: Aug. 12, 1888. . . . Yesterday P.M., we and the G. W. Chadwicks (he a musical composer who is distinctly bright; she, very pretty), John

To the Revd. H. W. Fay

Preston, also musical, Clayton Johns, likewise a devotee, and an English youth, all went to a lake 25 miles off, then took boat to Tutzing, where we drank beer, then descended a hill till supper time, and then back to inn garden where we ate and drank beer. . . . We passed by the place where the late king put on immortality. I had imagined that he did this in an artificial pond, but no, it was in a very pretty lake, 13 miles long and 2 or 3 broad, with the Alps in the background. I suppose the reason was that his system finally got full of caraway seeds and so he went mad. Small blame to him, for quite as bad as the English mint is the German caraway seed in boiled potatoes and cold beetroot. . . .

Back from an inferior concert, inferior, i.e., as to music, but most excellent as to beer. I find that the beergarden music no longer gives (Monday Aug. 13) the intense delight that it did 20 years ago. Such are the disadvantages, you see, of musical culture; one lives and cults and so prepares to bid a cheerful farewell to a disappointing world. . . .

Ritter, a musical painter, came here last evening. Miss Agnes Irwin is to arrive in a few days to stay here, being madly sold by Switzerland. The Chadwick man is distinctly bright. So shall I be, if I succeed in my present plan of learning Russian. I began it a few days ago and am, like our queen and empress, progressing finely. Whether I shall ever be able to read it is another question. My teacher kept me on "old table", "red floor" and such abominations, but today I struck for serious work and got on nobly. Drat their crazy letters, however! . . .

I have been interrupted 2 or 3 thousand times, and last evening, I went with C. Johns to see a German translation of *Le Monde où l'on s'ennuie.* It was very well given and is an amusing play but the men lacked the easy grace of the French when they saluted and clanged their heels together on entering a room, being introduced, etc. But that is a trifle; the whole thing was good! . . .

Paris: Feb. 13, 1889. . . . I read another curious novel of Lerocque's, *Odile,* with amazement. There is a wonderful amount of skill goes into the work of these fellows, but a Frenchman *can't* be a naturalist, altho' no race talks more about naturalization, just as liberty is a common aspiration and subject of conversation here where there is very little of the article, singularly little. Thus at the Bois the other day, tho' the ice was strong enough, every one was forbidden to go on ice; one skater ventured on in absence of police, and when he saw them coming he rushed to shore, and took off his skates as intimidated as if he had been laying dynamite bombs in front of a Ministry. And as to naturalism, a Frenchman is, above all things, an idealist; for isn't logic an ideal? This harms their scientific work, and compels them to see in facts an idea to which their minds cling, and any perversity in the fact has to be ignored. They have the merit of

To the Revd. H. W. Fay

not being hypocrites, but that consoles them for everything. . . .

On the whole, the Frenchman is a wonderful being and I can well understand the German's feeling as he does about him. I do not admire him as Brownell does. I have, as it were, been thro' that stage, and now I don't loathe him, but I don't, oh! I don't love him to the exclusion of every other man. For some of the Germans I saw this summer I felt real affection, notably for [Leopold von] Schroeder, because he knew more on certain things than any man I ever met, and yet was modest and anxious to learn about things he did not know; and if you by argument convinced him of anything, he stayed convinced. That work was done once for all and you did not have to do it over again. But no Frenchman is modest; he is sure that he knows everything better than you do, altho' he is too polite to show it directly; he will not listen to you if you say anything; he despises you, very civilly, if you don't acknowledge his superiority, and you can never convince him because he won't hear you. Of course we are brothers of the Germans and understand each other readily, and there is so much loose matter in our minds and ways of tho't that the Frenchman, who never makes any shavings or wastes the bone of a muttonchop, is repelled by our wayward mode of thinking and arguing, but he remains, in my opinion, hopelessly narrow. The garden which the Frenchman cultivates is a 7 x 9 kitchen garden, and, I may add, it is very well manured. He gives that part of horticulture his personal attention. . . .

Paris: Feb. 16. . . . Yes, Flaubert was a great man, and a wonderful realist as the critics say. Speaking of critics, I bought yesterday on the quais the works of Père Rapin, 2 vols. 12 mo. 1686, for 2 fr., and read much in them last night. I had never seen his writings before and they interested me much; he is a very clever man, after the principles of 2 centuries ago, and still very readable. Then I bought the volume of E. Hennequin just out, on Heine, Poe, Dickens, and the Russians, also good; tho' he, a boasted scientific critic, divides his men into idealists and realists and contrasts them confusedly, to my thinking, tho' much that he says is very good. But salvation is to be found only in observing the chronological belongings of a man; this is, of course, not merely the *dates,* but also the place where a man belongs. This does not, naturally, tell everything, but it is a *sine qua non* of sound criticism, and he overlooks it entirely. I wish that he had lived and that I might have seen him.

Paris: Feb. 20. Yesterday I shopped, the only Louvre I entered being the *Magasins* of that name, which many excellent American women mistake for the only Louvre there is. . . . We dine at the ——s. They have a dull grudge against us for not seeking their society and punish us by an invitation sent so

To the Revd. H. W. Fay

long beforehand that refusal is impossible. Whether they mean to scold us tonight or to put poison in our soup, I know not, but our social recalcitrance has been the subject of much wrathful discussion. . . . At any rate, I have always regarded society as an invention of stupid people to get bright people to entertain them. Now, having blown my little blast, I will go on. Observe Nestor in today's *Echo,* on lassitude. You will never, I know, believe me, but only yesterday I was thinking that what the French want more than anything else *is peace.* Call the government by any name, only let it be firm and quiet. They don't want to be forever bothered, but to be allowed to tend to their business and pleasure. They imagine that they will have a chance under Boulanger. Read also Jules Simon in *Le Matin* whose remarks lead up to this conclusion, altho' he doesn't state it. What other explanation can there be of this tolerance of this enormous charlatan? At any rate, the state of things, tho' painful, is interesting, and this trouble about the ministry is *very* dangerous, in my opinion. I think—but you know I am always wrong—that B. may move any day. But what a country it is. The impression of rot and decay that one gets here, is most terrible. Europeans call the Americans decadent. Heavens, let them look into their own looking-glasses. What strikes me more than anything else here is the physical degeneracy of the race. The men are short, weak, ugly, and unhealthy; the women are seldom pretty and often terribly crooked; the chil-

Thomas Sergeant Perry

dren are etiolated and dwarfed.—There's a little boy in the house; M. asked me to guess his age; I said 10. He is 14, and she or even Edith could throw him out of the window. But it is not kind to abuse one's hosts, as I seem to be doing in this letter. . . .

VI

(To John T. Morse, Jr.)

Karuizawa: Aug. 22, '00. ... You meanwhile have been disporting yourself with Zola. Yes, I have read the *Abbé Mouret,* but without admiration. I count it as one of his failures. It's convenient to have one man to bear the blame that belongs to a whole nation and so we call Zola nasty. It's only for convenience; he is unmistakably a great man with a bad name, just as Balzac was when I was young, and Miss Wormley, who has since translated all of B., was my Sunday School teacher (a fact). We had neither of us become acquainted with the great romancer then. It was in the spring of 1860, coming up the Mississippi in the steamboat *Peytona,* that I read my first of his work: *Le Colonel Chabert.* But I was saying it's now Zola who has all the blame for foulness of speech. You don't do the man justice; he has lying deep in his nature a keen love of propriety that almost amounts to prudishness. You know he went to England, and since he started with only the clothes on his back he was obliged to buy a new outfit, and what do you suppose most ruffled the peachy down of Emile's modesty? You would never guess: it was the brevity of English shirttails! You doubtless never bought any ready-made shirts in France—the idea of your buying a ready-made shirt anywhere is supremely ridiculous! I did once in '91, and I thought they would never wear out. They seemed to be made of such canvas as once carried our clippers triumphant round Cape Horn. They represented a bulging front, but so do most shirts in France, where once I sat flat as a tombstone and alone in that distinction at the Opera, when a lady, whom I shall never, never forget, found a way to the heart palpitating in the immediate neighborhood of that snowy slab, and said, with most winning tact: "Mr. Perry, yours is the only shirt front in the whole house that doesn't bulge!" But that was one of Keep's efforts. When you have 25 francs to spend in Paris for a shirt, you don't, like me, go to a linendraper's just below my apartment but you cross the rue de Castiglione and get measured by Doucet; so you are ignorant of the enfolding length of the national shirt of France, which seems to be based on the rustic blouse. It was to that Zola was accustomed, and he blushed to see himself standing in the bobtail production of England, to which we in our Anglomania are hardened. Zola—it's a way he has—expressed his sentiments in print, and I saw that he was not wholly lost. . . .

Tokyo: Sept. 19, '00. . . . It seems to me that you much misinterpret M.S. [Moorfield Storey] by begrudging him his unhappiness about affairs. It is that unhappiness which is the salvation of a country.

To John T. Morse, Jr.

A man can't carry a heavy load of responsibility as jauntily as he would swing a bamboo-cane. The condition is serious—is always serious—to condemn M.'s indignation is like laughing at the hurry of firemen on a hot day. No! I thank God there is some one left to be indignant, to be cross, if necessary, to disturb smugness by growling. Because in America we become rich easily, is it to be supposed that we can avoid all the troubles which have made the world? Not a bit of it; the old Devil is waiting for us yet. The fight must always go on. We lay down after the war with a sense of duty performed which was to carry at least us, of our time, to honoured graves. (I remember, as I have often told you, how M. S. regretted being born to ignoble times, when there was nothing to do, the devil was handcuffed and muzzled; it was at one of our club dinners, some 30 yrs. ago). But, as you heard last Sunday, at King's Chapel (if you worship there) the Old Man isn't dead yet. Those who inform you of this painful fact are annoying; so is the servant who tells you that your expensive roof leaks, that your house burns, etc., etc., etc. Thank Heaven that there is an honest man yet on the footstool to make a row. You have been unjust to M. Of course there are vast and starry stretches which go on with a certain monotony whether McKinley or Bryan is elected (that is really the amusing part of the whole business), but, just as time, as a man's life, consists of a series of 5-minute periods, these stretches are made up of a series of imminent duties such as those M. S. reminds us of. It's a comfort to see a man like that, a man who *is,* and not a man playing with life. Most people are part of a crowd.

Paris: Nov. 11, '05. It is a great pleasure to be in a country where food is treated with proper respect. Thus at home it is impossible to have spinach properly cooked unless one pays to the ministering angel a large salary—and not always then. Here the humblest of slaves cooks it as the good Lord meant it should be cooked. M. and her mother suffered untold tortures from English cookery, from the reckless profusion of cabbage, the absence of all decent nutriment. E. and I arranged a delicate meal for them on their arrival; string beans, a bird, grapes and pears; such were the leading members of the feast, and the change was most noteworthy and gratifying. Yet, so mysterious are the ways of Providence, this culinary skill, which is one of the brightest ornaments of France, is one source of its weakness. It is one of the little ties that (as happened to Gulliver) binds the Frenchman to his soil and makes him incapable of living elsewhere. The Englishman is glad to leave home, he can't feed worse anywhere else and so he conquers the world. The Frenchman must have his soup, his minced spinach, his artichokes, his red wine. The Englishman rushes to strong drink, the Frenchman's strong drinks are horrid! You won't find this point made by my rival philosopher,

To John T. Morse, Jr.

Emerson, but his incompetence is only proved by this omission. . . .

Nov. 24, 1905. . . . I have spoken to you with, I hope, not unbecoming fervour of the merits of French cooking, but I feel it my duty (in view of the biography which you are doubtless writing, so as to get out the first one) to tell you that I am not a blind and ignorant admirer of their skill. There is one thing of theirs of which they are very proud that I can't swallow and that's their *beastly* coffee. They will roast it to death and brew a bitter decoction from the ashes which is without any faintest flavour of the delicious berry. . . . Just think of it, in my short life compelled to give up cigars and coffee, because both are so poor! Smoking tobacco is not yet impaired and will probably last my time. These French cheeses are better than ever. Tho' imitation red wine abounds, it is possible to get the genuine and good, but to lose coffee and cigars, not in obedience to the foolish advice of a physician who is kept awake by them and revenges himself in that very unfair manner, but because the real stuff can't be got, it's hard. . . .

Jan. 27, 1906. A little matter has just arisen which, I hope, will not lead to any international complications or, what is worse, to any intestine troubles. It is this. I was sitting this morning reading my paper when a card was brought to me and I was told that the gentleman was in the next room. The name on the card was M. Fallières, the next president. I went in and after the usual formalities at meeting a President, he saying *"Enchanté"* as I wrung his hand, he speedily came to the nub of his visit. He said that he was taking this great step, leaving private life, that he should have to entertain much, that Mme. F.'s health was delicate, she is not so young as she was once, and he felt the necessity of getting some help, and well, he had heard about my cook and wanted me to let him take her.

I objected that of course I supposed, while I should gladly oblige him in any possible way, that there was a cook established in the Elysée who was a permanency and didn't go out, like a postmaster with us, when a new president came in. He explained that M. Loubet was taking the cook with him and he wanted the place filled by my cook and by no one else.

I was polite (as I always am to my betters) but very firm (what M. F. calls impolite) and said that I did not see my way clear, etc., and we parted with the question still unsettled. He said he would send, to press the matter further, one of his ministers, I suppose the Minister of the Interior. So there it stands. Our cook has retired behind the battery *de cuisine* to await the outcome of the struggle between me and the autocracy of France. . . .

Feb. 1, '06. Last evening we went, all of us, to the Français to see Musset's *Les Caprices de Marianne,*

To John T. Morse, Jr.

which, if you don't know by heart, read. It will give a pleasant taste to your mouth after Ibsen, tho' you had the great advantage of hearing him in Russian and so of not understanding a word. In that way he appears to have made a great impression on you. I confess that I have not been carried off my feet as delicate souls tell me I ought to be. I have been exposed to most dangerous draughts of Ibsenian zeal, in Germany, here, at home, but have so far escaped the fever. I have had only the chill. I read him with tepid interest, but the trouble is that I can't see in his plays all that people tell me is there: judgment of society, condemnation of everything. I am too stupid. I can only see, and that blindly, what is put before my eyes. I don't read well between the lines. When Hedda Gabler gabbles, she seems to me an insufferable nuisance, a mass of conceit and wrongheadedness. If that's the woman of the future, I'm glad I'm living now. If she is a Scandinavian, give me a Patagonian. This is one enthusiasm, Ibsenism, that I have managed to escape. I think his plays, some of them, pretty good, but as for revelations from on high and all that, dear me, dear me! If you want to read a great play, read Tolstoy's *Puissance des Ténèbres*. . . .

March 6, 1907. . . . I have been down to the valley of the shadow of Obituaries. I lay very ill, all had given me up and I was slowly drifting into that region which you have made so peculiarly your own, when I remembered what a fist you would make of it writing about me and clambered back. The experience is not wholly without interest, and then it gives me at least an opportunity to get back at the millions of people who have spent so much of their time in telling me about their typhoids, yellow fevers, carbuncles, surgical operations of various sorts, etc., etc. Hitherto I have been compelled to confine myself to such bald platitudes as: "Very sorry," "Yes, but I hope it's better now," "Sad indeed, but you really ought to be careful what you eat," "It's too bad, but if no one were sick, what would become of the poor doctors?" "Terrible, but I can't understand what pleasure there is in wearing pumps a size too small," etc. You know the sort of phrase that rises at once to the lips of a mildly sympathetic but truly highbred gentleman in such cases. Then they had me and went on with their sufferings. You see, since Feb. 1862 I had nothing the matter with me till Feb. 25 of this year, 45 yrs. . . . Was I grateful for this immunity? Not in the least. Who was ever grateful for anything? I wasn't going to be ridiculous even if I had felt a faint twinge of gratitude. Now at last I have a crushing answer ready when any one opens fire on me with an account of falling downstairs, from a balloon, or any of these tiresome stories. I shall annihilate them with a long and full, very full, account of my Grippe. Don't start and turn away with impatience, I may try it on you yet. You see it wasn't the ordinary snuffling, barking

To John T. Morse, Jr.

grippe such as most people make so absurd an ado about. It was a grippe quite apart. *Grippa regum,* that seized me. The noxious poison entered my stalwart system by the foulest treachery and went straight for the citadel where dwelt in apparent security the commander, General Appetite, and smote him a deadly blow. Then he telephoned to the trusty Digestive Organs, commanding them to take a few days off. They asked, "Who gave that order?" "I'm the Walking Delegate," he answered, while he called up the Liver, bade it dampen its fires, take off its pipes.

You may imagine your Uncle Thomas's perturbation, no sign of grippe, no apparent cause for the horrid anarchy. Had he been poisoned? Tempting dishes were placed before him. They might have been thrown into the street. Doctors were haled in and Science appeared Baffled. An appetite unbroken for 45 years lay dead before them or in a mortal swound. They searched me for typhoid, but no, it was my kind of grippe, and so I was put to bed. This was Wednesday last. Monday morning I woke with a sense of freedom. That excellent sudorific Aspirin (per aspirin ad astra) caught the Foul Fiend when he was wandering about my frame in search of an untouched Vital Organ, and swept him away. Gradually I have crawled back to health. Gen'l Appetite, who was supposed to be dead, had merely fainted and the application of a few stimulants, principally strychnine, has brought him back to life, not only unimpaired but even sharper than ever. Food, once loathed, is now yearned for. I wish you were living near me to send in about a dozen eggs a day and a chicken or two for my convalescences. . . .

Feb. 24, 1908. Your welcome valentine reaches me this morning and my Cadbury's cocoa which I am forced to drink on account of the worthlessness of French coffee, grew cold while I read your entertaining pages. I am glad the club dinner thrives. I am glad that you are reading Ferrero. You will find more novelty as you go on, and what surprised me was the abundance of it in view of the way the period had been gone over. Its main quality seems to me to be his treatment of the subject as if it were modern history, the way he illustrates it from our times. It was very interesting to meet F. and to see how his mind works. It is not hidden in his book, but his talk brought it out more readily.

Saturday I went to the American ambassador's Feb. 22 reception to leave long-delayed cards. He has just moved into a very palatial hotel which was crammed with our country people. We met Mrs. Wolcott and her daughter and brought them round from that gorgeous palace to our plain New England home for a cup of tea. Mrs. W. told me something that had just happened to her there, and tho' there is nothing meaner than telling another person's stories, I reflect that perhaps she will have forgotten

To John T. Morse, Jr.

it when she gets home and it's a pity it should be lost. There was, you will understand, a great rabble there. Mrs. Wolcott asked Mrs. White if she could be of any service to her. Mrs. White said if you see any lone, lorn thing, hopelessly stranded, won't you go to her relief? As Mrs. Wolcott was going through the gilded drawing-rooms, her eye fell on a faded frump of a woman, who looked like a dressmaker's assistant who had saved just money enough to take advantage of the new low steamship rates, and so, full of Christian charity, she made her way through the gorgeous throng to the sad waif. She opened fire by asking her if she didn't think the rooms very fine. "Oh, yes," was the answer, "it's a very nice house. We thought of taking it ourselves, but we found something we liked better.". . .

Feb. 25, '08. . . . By the way the Abbé Loisy's book on the *Synoptiques,* 2 vols. 30 fr. might interest you. It's awfully good reading, I am sure. Then, too, now that you have got your shelves somewhat free, why don't you treat Mrs. Morse to that new edition of H. James's *Opera omnia?* Not only do I want to save this generation from the odium of neglecting its best writers, but I also want to entertain her. You ought to do it . . . and H. J. sells 750 copies of his *American Scene,* a great book which we sneer at because it is at first sight a little hard to read. If you expect me to entertain for you any feeling of respect, you must do as I say. . . .

Thomas Sergeant Perry

March 12, 1908. I have your letter of the 2nd. Before I begin further comment, let me ask what in the world you mean by objecting to French dinners. . . . You speak the language of insanity. What do you mean by "too much coarse meat"? Is it beef? We never have it in the house. Is lamb a coarse meat? Chicken? Game? You appear to think that we live on pork and pigs' trotters. It's the second time that you have made this absolutely incoherent statement. Too much cheese! Too much for whom? Do you know what French cheese is? "French dinners lacking in refinement." Whenever you get tired of them you can go down town and get a boiled dinner. I have run across in my reading from time to time various rash and unfounded statements but never the mate of this.

The rest of your letter is more marked with intelligence and the fruits of civilization. . . .

St. Petersburg: May 21, June 3, 1908. . . . As you see we are still in St. P. The only thing worth seeing is the Hermitage with its very beautiful pictures. We also enter mildly into the alleged joys of social life. The other night the Austrian Ambassador, Count Berchtold and his charming wife dined here; Saturday we dine at the American Ambassador's, etc., and then Sunday we propose moving to the seaside, but these particulars are of no interest. Let me turn rather to the new degree, D.C.V., Dr. of Civic Virtue, abt. to be given to favorite sons. A wise pre-

To John T. Morse, Jr.

caution would be to give it as one gives scholarships and fellowships, for a brief term, but anyway it would be ridiculous. Since say the Revolution, and before, the usual honorary degrees have been given to prominent men, to Washington, LaFayette, and others not renowned for scholarship, to many governors, etc. Why change? It looks like some one's attempt to bring Harvard College nearer the great heart of the nation, whereas it is most desirable to keep as many important things as possible untainted by politics. That comparative cleanliness helps to give them weight. Already there have been traces (and very distinct traces) of the college serving strictly political ends, but this new degree would be rank exhibition of this tendency. I agreed with you perfectly about it, but we are too wise for this world, which is the reason that we shall soon be transferred to a more congenial one.

In fact, this giving of honorary degrees wearies me. At about this time in the year begins the hunt for a man to work in your garden and another to get a degree. The proper authorities read long lists of say "divines" and other worthies who have lived 50 odd years without appearing in a police-court and thus are the joys of Commencement thoughtfully prepared well in advance. The gentleman who declined such shopworn honours alone deserves them.

You see how wise I am, how I live in a beautiful ivory tower and audibly and odiously sniff at my kind. You might read this letter to Rev. Hale (E.E.) and get him going on the subject at Commencement. He will amuse you. The conclusion of the whole matter is this: that the only thing which succeeds in this world is believing in something which you know can't be so, can't be true. I need not point out how immensely true this is in religion—try the doctrine of the Trinity for example, then patriotism, the whole social system. When everybody has attained our exalted height of pure truth, this civilization will necessarily end and a new one, arranged probably on the political systems of an ant-hill, will prevail, but we shan't be here. . . .

Hancock, N. H., Oct. 4, 1910. Do you want a horse for the winter? It may be that your stable is full of champing steeds, but if not let me call your attention to a noble horse who has been working for us all summer and for whom we want to find a careful home for the winter in a Christian family. His name is John Hancock, he is a capital roadster, and really without fault. He is absolutely indifferent to the snorting motor-car and is indeed a really commendable beast. Can you have any use for such aN (notice the common, mock elegant aN) one? If so we will trust J. H. to you till May 1 with perfect confidence. But I suppose you have more horses than you want. You need have no fear that this is an unworthy one, for he is a beauty, chosen for us by Ned Burnett, and speedy as the Back Bay wind. . . . I will not weary you with importunities for

To John T. Morse, Jr.

all my more or less dumb beasts, but I do ask about the hoss.

July 23, 1915. . . . As for the Germans, their whole point of view is that they want to torpedo right and left. What sort of an excuse is it that it was after sunset and they couldn't see the name of the ship? Another time the captain will have some salt water or an eyelash in his eye and we shall be expected to hold that a valid excuse. As a matter of fact, they not only hate, they despise us, and feel sure that we will never do anything to them, and for this state of mind they are indebted to Herr von Bryan. When his talk with Dumba becomes public property, you will see how naturally the impression spreads among the German authorities—or I'm a Dutchman, like v. B. himself. . . . I have never, 'till this last year, appreciated the great civilising value of chivalry, about which so much has been written, but now I see its importance. I have always wanted to write a history of manners, but the subject is too vast for any one man not a German, and no German knows anything whatever about the subject, though that never bothers him. . . .

August 13. . . . Did you notice that the Berlin papers *say* that the *Hymn of Hate* and *Gott Straf' England* motto are going out of fashion? If this statement is true, it is—as I just wrote to Alice—the first sign that their reason is returning, but, as I also

Thomas Sergeant Perry

remarked to her, it will take more than that to make us feel for a long time that a German is a fellow-being. How much they have to live down! And the curious thing is that they will try to brazen and bluster it out as they have always done. Perhaps they are right—the world will forget their charming qualities, just as nature will hide the battlefields and people will admire their wonderful efficiency once more, and then if their manners are a little rough, it's only because they are so sincere and frank. It's the easiest thing in the world to forget. Look at France, what a lesson she had. You would think she knew what the Germans are, but those who knew and said what they knew, were looked upon as public nuisances. It's really just as hard to be wise after the event as before. . . . You speak with characteristic violence of the weather and the consequent mosquitoes. Against these last plagues we have screened doors and windows, and to repel those who pass these barriers (we have even our chimneys topped with screens), we have Mosquitaway, bottles of which S. S. Pierce supplies. It is really oil of cedar, which those odious insects detest. . . . I have killed at least a million. They don't bother me much. They approach my massive frame, soaked with rum and tobacco, taste one drop of my poisoned blood and fall to the ground writhing in agony. Wasps bother me very little, I suppose on the principle that dog doesn't eat dog. . . . But what a year for mushrooms! I unfortunately can't eat them, having once been nearly

To John T. Morse, Jr.

swept off the face of the earth after partaking of a most savory mess.

August 31. Your noble letter of the 29th crossed mine of yesterday. I haven't read Hadley on Treitschke, but you need have no fear in thinking all that his enemies say. I can show you enough German testimony to that effect to bury Hadley completely under. Thus I remember what Paulsen said of him as quoted in his Life, and others have agreed with him. The fact is, he was mad about the greatness of Germany. All the rest of the world he hated, and England especially because it was rich and free. Freedom he abhorred. The freedom that England has was to him something like free love, or free lunch. Consider only the things quoted from him and they would warrant hanging him. . . . Why you have no props to sustain your anti-German sentiments I don't clearly see. . . . If you have nothing against the Germans, except their table manners, you are a very singular person. Do you think that Germany began the war in self-defense, that the tearing of treaties, the invasion of Belgium is nothing? Do you approve of her methods of fighting? But of course you don't mean what you say. . . . I have a most interesting book: *Histoire de l'Invasion Allemande en 1870-1871,* par le Général F. Canonge. Perrin. 1915. You would say after reading it that the French had enjoyed ample opportunity to learn exactly what the Germans are and would never be caught again, but they came very near. They did then most all the things they have done in this war, though I must be fair and confess that this wonderful race has advanced where advance seemed impossible. That I suppose is what you admire in them. If you have gone so far as really to have nothing against the Germans but a certain prejudice, let me know. . . .

September 7. . . . What you say of —— interests me. I used to know him, say forty years ago, and we discovered that we had actually nothing in common, not one taste or interest. What he liked I had no fancy for, and he was building himself a resting-place within such thick walls of prejudice that I couldn't touch him. I never saw such conservatism as he proclaimed. I have not had six words with him for certainly thirty-five years, nor shall I. We shall never meet, though I used to enjoy fighting with him in the old days. As for Root, thanks for his speech, which is excellent. . . . He is of course a very able and very wise man, and it is very strange that he has risen so high in spite of those obstacles. Care has been taken that he should not rise too high. He is just the sort of man that a democracy hates. I am glad to see you trying to clear yourself from the terrible charge of pro-Germanism. I can't exactly follow the delicate arguments that prove the existence of another German nation innocent of all the things that the German nation is doing, or at least the Germans

To John T. Morse, Jr.

who constitute the nation. The statement is made at times, but it is never clear to me. I am glad Germany has a higher self. I wish it would put it to some practical use. . . . You are perfectly right in speaking of the Europeans as you do. They are superior to us in very many ways, and that is why I like to live there. I have a chance to pick up crumbs of greater interest than the stock market reports. The American is a less interesting human being. We are a crude, ignorant, half-baked, absurdly conceited lot. Of course I infinitely prefer living there, among human beings. Yet there are worse places than these where we gnaw our chains. We have staying with us a lady, born and brought up in Paris, who has been living for some years in Wichita, Kansas! She likes the place in some ways, but what a dreary note it must be and how the great middle west must roar with the buzz of beings *bombinans in vacuo*. No wonder they are ready to admire Bryan. Why, on one of the plains on which they live, a lilac bush would seem a monarch of the forest. The state is full of piety (so-called), every other man a deacon or a Sunday-school teacher, but when you go away you have to leave some one in the house or the doors and windows and all that is within them would be stolen as a matter of course. They all do their own work in that happy land. You have tendencies that way and will sympathise with them. I get an impression of dreariness. The plains must be very plain. I don't dare to start any statement of what I really think of life in this country. I should find myself writing a book that would be burned by the public hangman. . . . I am amused by Bethman-Hollweg's comparatively recent attacks on England. The Germans must think us awful fools to give us such stuff. They see that their own people will swallow anything their leaders choose to give them and imagine us just as credulous and docile. After all, it perhaps is wise to suppose the world to be full of fools, but in time the truth gets out. . .

September 15. . . . What you say of all countries, that they are always actuated by pure selfishness, reminds me of the utterances of those gentlemen who prove that all human actions, and especially those most generally admired, are only manifestations of that unlovely quality; thus, a man saves a person drowning at the risk of his own life, not because he wants to do a kindness, but because he prefers that act to possible remorse if he didn't do it, and perhaps wanted a cold bath anyway. You know the arguments, schools of philosophy have been built and run on that foundation. . . .

September 24. . . . The other day there occurred to me this definition: Life is the process of forming habits, mostly bad ones. I am vain enough to think it better than the classic definition of life: One damned thing after another! A Sunday might be profitably

To John T. Morse, Jr.

spent in considering this, my utterance, but no, you will do nothing of the sort. . . .

September 29. . . . I wanted to send you a merry note of welcome to town to meet you on your arrival, thus lessening your agony at leaving the beauteous country, but you will be thinking of other things and notably of poor ——'s loss. It will be a sad blow for him, and I am really sorry for him. That is what one gets for living. Instead of getting nicely out of the way and leaving everyone to think of how much you would have done if only you had been spared, one lives and loses everyone. I went to Dublin yesterday in my little Ford and saw Pumpelly. You who are fond of nature and views and such things do well not to come here, for I have no wider view than expands before me at 312 [Marlborough Street, Boston]. If I want a view I am grateful for a sufficient inducement to going out, and having reached the appropriate spot gaze at remote spots, uttering suitable adjectives for about three or five minutes, when I begin to think of other things and either go on with my walk or come back home. But Pumpelly is perched on a high hill dividing the Connecticut and Merrimac valleys—don't be afraid, I'm not going to describe the view save in the most general terms, i.e., that it is most wide, with a lake below, which it would be an insult to call a pond, though so it was called until summer visitors seemed to enlarge it with the new name.—By the way, isn't it properly

Thomas Sergeant Perry

Wood's Hole? Isn't *Hole* the real and customary name all along the coast for such snug harbours? . . .

October 4. . . . Did you ever know anything like the Fate of some people? Ordinary persons pick out a day and then the course of nature runs on without interruption. It is not so with me. I set a date and then all the Forces of the Universe get to work to make just those twenty-four hours impossible. It shows how important I am, what significance has my every action! . . .

July 3, 1916. . . . Anecdote from Dublin (N. H.). A multi-millionaire from Chicago said to the Rev. Basil King, one day after service, "Did you know that you were preaching today to (17-100-200-or whatever it was) millions?" He had better look out or B. K. will get him into one of his novels. Mrs. —— complained to a friend of mine: "You know how hard it is to get rid of your money." He didn't know. . . . Dublin is a beautiful spot, but living there must be very trying. . . .

July 18. Your adventure with the eagle thrilled and alarmed me. It was certainly most interesting; only the other day someone asked me if any were seen nowadays in these parts and I had to confess that they were rare. In all my adventurous life I have seen, I think, only one in freedom, and that was many years ago. Of late they have become as rare as the roc.

To John T. Morse, Jr.

. . . You explain your fear by supposing that you were to be snatched away like a kid or a lamb and carried away to feed a lot of eaglets. Nonsense, you escaped a much greater danger. You came near being carried off like Ganymede. That was what I feared. Doubtless all-knowing Zeus has heard of your cocktails. How curious it would have been if that had happened! It would have been telegraphed and cabled all over the world. . . . Your devout friends would have insisted that like Enoch of old you were translated, but in this scientific age the truth would have come out soon. I don't know in exactly what terms I should have spoken about it in the contributor's page of the *Transcript*. Precedents there are, but too remote for practical use. . . . I hope you will be careful when you go off on these excursions when the air becomes a new element of danger, as the water always was. Carry a gun with you, loaded with buck-shot. Can it be that those recent fearful thunder-storms are signs of Jove's just wrath at being defrauded of his prey? It looks like it. Be careful at all times. You can't think how glad I am that you have had your verandah fenced in. . . . I was so taken up by the thought of you as Ganymede that though I had your letter open before me, I was guilty of the atrocious crime with which I understand you are sometimes charged. I forgot to answer your question about the birthplace and genealogy of the polyandrous Donna Julia who preferred four husbands at twenty-five to one of one hundred or par.

Thomas Sergeant Perry

That indelicate person does not stain the innocent pages of *Don Giovanni*. The opera treats rather of the polygamous adventures of its hero. But aren't you perhaps thinking of the Donna Julia in the *Don Juan* of the gifted but frail Lord Byron? It sounds like him. I have not the poems of Byron here, nor are they in the town library, so you must look it up yourself. . . .

August 4. . . . I hate to think of you exposed to a Sabbath without a letter from me to hold you in the right path. You so seldom go to church and so often neglect books of piety, that I can't leave you uncared for, though I have nothing to say. As I remember it, parsons never used to let that excuse keep them silent. The less they had to say, the longer they went on. I was meant by nature to be a parson. That sanctimonious aspect was thrown away on a scoffer. You didn't see the prophecies published in France and recounted in the *Transcript* of Wednesday. They are the best sort of prophecies, written after the event. It's wonderful what good work can be done in that way; and since in the eyes of philosophy there is no such thing as *time,* what difference does it make? These prophecies which are not half so good as Wells' in his novels, are sent out without a proof, very naturally, for no proofs exist, of their genuineness. If they were genuine, they wouldn't be half so precise. You can't have everything. Something must be sacrificed and we get the best part. . . .

To John T. Morse, Jr.

August 11. . . . In an illegible postscript I spoke very briefly of the onslaught of the Fire King, armed with Jove's thunder-bolt, upon the barn and house of goodman —— on the Bennington road. Poor man, he lost all he had in the world. He had painfully accumulated a few hundred dollars and had bought this $1,300 farm with a $600 mortgage and worked on the railway. When he saw the house burning he wanted to perish with it and shut himself up in a closet, but his neighbours dragged him out by force. His wife and children, as I told you, were at Antrim for the day. It was just as well, for thereby the horse was saved, and for that matter Mrs. —— too, for she, it seems, had a great dread of thunderstorms and used to run to the barn—of all places—when one approached. Had she done this the other day, she would have been killed. When they got back from Antrim, they found what had happened to their new home in the village. All Hancock has subscribed to give the poor fellow another start. Such is the gloomy tale of life on our granite hills. . . .

August 15. . . . Hesiod, if I remember right, warns against setting out tomatoes in a vanishing moon. To that store of folk-lore I can add one maxim —don't undertake to let your cat sleep inside at the full of the moon. I tried it the other night, taking pity on its having to sleep beneath the verandah with a temperature of 48 degrees, and at bed-time called it in and took it to my room. You, with your wide

[85]

experience of kittens, will at once not ask—you are too polite for that—but wonder how the little animal was at once house-broken. I will pass over the details very lightly and merely say that the little housebreaker might have been brought up in the family of a refined plumber, so neat were its habits, so quick its appreciation. . . . This kitten was born with a perfect comprehension of the whole matter. . . . The real trouble was that the kitten was so delighted at being brought from the, as it were, ash-hill to the abode of comfort and culture, that it couldn't close an eye for hours. It sprang in the air in a vain attempt to catch its own tail and dropped all over me. It wandered my whole length, purred into my ears, tickled my cheeks with its whiskers and tried to get under the blankets, and kept me awake for hours, but at last it slept. . . .

August 26. . . . I am sorry to mar with a blot the expression of gratitude for the favours received by the poor burnt-outs. We are simple people, we Hancockers, or Hancockerels, but some of the rarer virtues still abound here. Gratitude is called a virtue, but I suppose only because it is so rare. I doubt if it rises to the high rank of *virtue;* it is more a piece of good manners. The Chinese don't thank you, any more than does a cat—of course I mean the Chinese coolies—and though the Jap does, it is only as a bit of manners. Then of course the intelligent sense of favours to come is the great source of gratitude. No,

To John T. Morse, Jr.

the natural state of man feels that whatever good comes to him is simply the inevitable result of natural laws for which it is merely polite to show gratitude. We don't thank the sun for shining. On the other hand, anything that goes wrong seems like a gross perversion of natural laws, and we are indignant. I think, too, that perhaps the rarity of gratitude is a mercy. The other day someone was positively grateful to L. and me—I forget for what, nothing of any importance—but the appearance of this almost nonexistent quality was anything but pleasing; it was indeed quite harrowing. I said to L.: "This only shows that it is really a mercy that gratitude is so rare. Instead of regretting this, we should be grateful ourselves." To be consistent, we should not be grateful, so will say we should be "very pleased.". . .

August 27. . . . I see that patriot Henry L. Higginson proposes to take advantage of the regular and unbroken course of time to urge putting up permanent exposition buildings on small islands in the basin of the Charles. What small islands does he mean? I recall none, so I suppose he means to create them. Why is it that there are some men who can't see a body of water without wanting to litter it up with islands, just as their mates can't see a big tree without wanting to cut it down? Henry is not alone in this turpitude. ——, who combines with an overflowing enthusiasm for all sorts of follies a church higher than Rome on a show day, devotion to the

Thomas Sergeant Perry

last Charles I, slavish adoration of Gothic architecture . . . wrote to the *Transcript* two or three years ago a proposal to celebrate the arrival of the Pilgrims by putting up a lot of cathedrals, one for every sect, on these yet non-existing islands. He didn't confine himself to cathedrals, he wanted also a lot of music halls, lecture rooms, convention halls, athletic rinks, etc., all over the place. I meant to write an answer, but his proposition was so absurd that I really feared it was meant for a joke and needed no correction. I go back to my original question: Why islands? I know, sir, that you will tell me that there is in town no vacant land for proper buildings and will point out the horrid danger of jobs if one should buy anywhere with the public funds, but I am not convinced of the advantage of putting up a new museum that will be forever shrieking for funds. All this celebration business seems to me ill-advised at this period of the world's history, and if I hear any more of this island building I shall write to Henry. There seems to be as great call for islands even as for shipping. The supply being short, it is proposed that we buy those belonging to Denmark, and our infant industries add their manufacture to their long list of occupations. Sir, I ask you, have we not enough islands already? . . .

August 30. . . . I note the lofty tone of prophecy in your letter. You must understand that I am a good deal of a prophet myself. I am not in the least discouraged by never getting it right, any more than

To John T. Morse, Jr.

a gambler is by bad luck. I am a perfect Casabianca, or rather a Napoleon of prophecy, though I still think it is better to prophecy afterwards. You draw a dismal picture, I acknowledge, but you don't go far enough! You make Brandeis president in 1920, but you stop there. It is vouchsafed to me to see further, deeper into futurity, and while I see the country writhing under the thrall of that accomplished Jew, I see the rising of a great nation in behalf of a Christian saint and Cardinal O'Connell resigning from his sacred office and running against Brandeis, who yearns for a triumphant reëlection, not because he likes the job, but merely as a certificate of good faith. After eight years . . . I see a country united under a prominent German, named Münsterberg, who, winning all hearts, turns the country over to Germany—and then how sorry you will be that you never learned German, for it will be too late then, and you are no Cato. . . . Your programme is, I think, a very likely one. You say Hughes is uninspiring. He probably is, most presidents are. Lincoln was not, and Cleveland very nearly escaped the usual fate. The inspiring person is W. W., and he inspires everyone with the most intense dislike. It is he who keeps the Republican party going, not Hughes. . . .

September 21. . . . They sent me a personal letter begging for anything from $50 to $300, to aid in building the enclosed civic hall. (National Civic Hall, Washington). There was added a list of con-

Thomas Sergeant Perry

tributors from Massachusetts, and while many of my respectable friends shone there, Dudley Pickman, H'y Parkman, etc., at the letter *M* there was a most brilliant gap. I was surprised, for I should have supposed that you would have seen how necessary such a building is. Suppose, for instance, that you and I should hold different views on some question, instead of your filling your library with your sophisms while I could not get in a reasonable word edgewise, we should take the train for Washington, enter the Civic Hall and beat the matter out. After we had both said all we had to say, we could go to the hall devoted to reconciliation of views and become friends again. We shouldn't have to go to Washington to learn how to recognize abuses. Don't you think that such a hall would be cheap for two and a half millions (estimated)? What in the world is this building for anyway, except to give berths to an army of attendants? Who shall decide what orator speaks? And at this Chautauquans and cranks of all sorts? It will be like the Common of a pleasant Sunday afternoon, for it can be denied to no one, and in winter it will be a snug resort for the homeless. Yet E. Root wants it, or says he wants it. What for? Who has the job of building it? Who will have the job of "running" it? Who shall decide what orator speaks? And at this moment when there is an unceasing demand for every dollar that can be spared, we are to give $300 to this forum for fools. . . .

To John T. Morse, Jr.

September 26. . . . As for Thucydides and his suitability as historian of the present war, we must remember that the position of sophistical defender will have many applicants. There will be an army of them to prove that England, Russia, Montenegro, any land you please, began the war and that everything the Germans did was right and holy and the contrary of the Allies. The world will be swamped with those lying tales. Only professors can write history in Germany, and they are all sworn to defend the Kaiser and all his works. I sometimes wonder if our view of the Athenians is not in some sort the result of their careful loading of the histories. We have of Rome only the Roman accounts. An Etruscan or a Carthaginian history might throw some valuable light. See how absurdly the position of Great Britain has been represented in our histories, how in many the aid given by France has been left out. Nothing absurder can be imagined than the whole lot of these sources of information and inspirers of prejudice. . . . Bury's book on the historians is good. I too have read and forgotten it. The fact is he says so many good, wise things that one can't remember all. Then, too, one's thoughts seldom turn back to Herodotus and Thucydides, so one has no occasion to muse on what Bury said. I could read the book over again with profit; possibly I might exhume from my mind some of the things he said—I read it very recently, two or three years only ago—but not many.

Thomas Sergeant Perry

. . . The declining years of the late Mr. —— were soothed for him by an even greater deliquescence of the memory, so that instead of sending over to the Public Library for a new book, the morning *Advertiser* lasted him all day. By the time he had finished page eight, page one was again new, and so on. That is the reward of a long and useful life. . . .

October 5. . . . I have been looking at some numbers of the *New Republic*. They seem very eager to be progressive and democratic and American, but further I gather nothing. What specific changes they want is not clear, any more than what they mean by the American spirit. I don't think they know exactly what they do mean. What you say about the election interests me. It may be that Hughes by his flawless behavior, his discreet silences, is repelling faster than he attracts. I confess that I am impatient of his dumbness about the war. Here is the most important question before the world that there has been for years, and he says: "We must support the *American spirit*." . . . What a day this is and what days there have been! Nowhere else in the world is there such weather. In that respect the American spirit really means something. . . .

June 18, 1917. . . . That novel, *Le Feu,* is simply *terrible* because it is so damnably true. As I wrote to Howells, he makes Tolstoi sound as romantic as Victor Hugo. I have never read such a book, though it

To John T. Morse, Jr.

is not all horror any more than the soldier's life, even at the front, is all horror. There are capital scenes in it, full of humour, endurable pathos. It is a remarkable book, one that makes a mark on history. . . .

July 13. . . . To my mind there is not the slightest doubt that the world is made up of gifted beings and a rabble. Aristotle and others have said so and they are right. The existence of C—— in his present position is a proof, once more, of Aristotle's intelligence and mine, for you and I know and foresaw the crowd that put him in. Yet toward the deification of that rabble we are moving with accelerated velocity. We all know how foolish it all is, but we go on with the procession as if we approved. That is called the grand march of humanity. I don't think much better of the lordly leaders. . . . In fact, the rabble is interesting when you get to know it. I have never known a man who didn't know something better than I did —which is not saying much—who didn't have something in him that raised him in perhaps an insignificant respect above his kind. Of course you will understand that *never* and *no one* are mere expressions, not assertions, etc., etc., etc. . . .

July 17. . . . W. W.'s phrases don't seem to do him any harm, they are like the mistakes one makes in speaking a foreign language. "Peace without victory," what harm has that foolish phrase done him? This German rumpus is interesting. If the Crown

Prince gets into the saddle it may seem that the military power is winning, but the Crown Prince is no favorite outside of his ring, and he would be thrown out much sooner than his father. Thus the event may very well be only encouraging for us ardent friends of "democracy." Even among the military the Crown Prince is not admired for himself, but merely for what he expresses. No one feels respect or affection for him. All these things that we see before us mean the break-down of our civilization, such as it is. We did well to choose the time we did to live in. Prices were excessively high, but we got [here] in time to smoke good cigars, and our declining years are soothed by Gillette's safety-razor. We also had a fair chance at the game birds. Yes, John, if man ever was grateful, we have every reason to feel gratitude, though of course we don't. . . .

July 18. . . . By the way, I haven't thanked you for the *Hist. Rev.,* a dullish number. The historians take themselves much too seriously. I have but little respect for history, and when I read one, not often, I like to read one that is written entirely on my side. That is why I like Tacitus and Froude, and Macaulay. When the Goncourts said, "L'histoire est du roman qui a été; le roman est de l'histoire qui aurait pu être," they missed their chance of saying a good thing. It's really just the other way round. I have never seen any report of anything of which I knew the facts, that wasn't blundered over. More-

To John T. Morse, Jr.

over, I truly think that everything the mind of man can imagine has been done or is done (and a lot more, too). So I say it is history that records what might have been, and the facts get into the novels. This, you see, is perfect Hegelianism. Get it all off to O. W. H. the next time you see him—as your own, I need hardly say. He will be delighted and will think much more highly of you, will begin to respect you and hail you as a fellow-philosopher. . . .

July 21. . . . You won't suppose that I write to communicate any news, for I have none. Aristocratic Dublin has not deigned to visit us, and pursues its giddy pleasures with no thought for sterling worth in humble garb. I have been improving my time by growling at all the news, at W. W. for letting those women out of gaol, and at T. R. for saying—what can't be true—that he, too, is a firm believer in "extending" the suffrage, as if there were not enough idiot voters already. Then my heart cracks when I read of idiocy getting ahead in Russia, so that altogether my nervous system is in such a state that I can no longer read my Congressional Record in calmness. What a set of fools and knaves they have under one roof in Washington. . . . You will observe that the Germans are spreading abroad the notion imparted to you that the English preferred to have their fighting done for them. The German is a crafty person, and he is playing the game for all it is worth, here as well as in other countries. The only mistake he makes is an apparently impossible one: He exaggerates the gullibility of the human race. . . .

July 24. . . . Even as my brook, erstwhile a merry prattler, is now dumb, having swooned away these last days, so my stream of ink appears to have run into the sand. The brook, as the newspapers and recent Harvard graduates say, has "quit" running. (Except *back of, locate, I would like, gotten*—you know the story of W. Everett remonstrated with for throwing a dictionary at a boy—"But", said W. E., "he said *gotten*"—did I tell you this the other day—I hate most *quit*.) "Balance of" for *rest* does not delight me. . . . I am amused by the news from Washington—I mean the general state of affairs there. W. W. apparently sets before himself the duty of doing right without inflicting damage on the Democratic party. A narrower partisan the world has not seen. He may regard this as the only way of getting anything done and he may be right, but what a state of affairs it is! As for Congress—well, words fail me. . . . Perhaps, after all, you were right in grabbing the talk all those winters. If actuated by any absurd and obsolete notion of social duty, you had asked me to speak, my jaw would have dropped, I should have had nothing to say, and now what a grievance I have: that you gave me no chance! . . .

August 6. . . . As for events in a somewhat larger circle, it is interesting to see the beautiful actions of

To John T. Morse, Jr.

the Socialists in Russia. One would have thought that all possible methods of d—d foolishness had been long exhausted, but it was left for these monkeys to set a new fashion, to make a new record. The wilder their antics, the better for the Kaiser, they just nail his throne surer than ever. He can ask nothing more of fate than to give those men all the rope they want. And what a lesson, too, for the rest of the world of what such beliefs foster when the time for action comes. They act so that even Socialists can see what follies they commit. . . .

August 14. . . . The German's conduct is, unfortunately, only too credible. It's curious what a reputation they have made for themselves, and yet Kuno Meyer, who says the whole world hates the Germans, holds that this hate is wholly unreasonable. They can't see, apparently, that anything they do should seem detestable. . . . I do not admire Grant's political career, though I admire the man, poor fellow, naked in a wasp's nest. I am not surprised that he drank when he did. Who wouldn't have drunk, a broken, helpless man of thirty-eight in Galena, Illinois? Think of Grant's rise from that slough, and of Kerensky! Yet we say there is nothing in the papers—there is nothing in us. . . .

August 17. . . . I begin this letter without anything to say. I am like ——, the astronomer, who one evening deserted the observatory for the mad whirl of Cambridge society and asked to be introduced to a lady whom he thought beautiful. They carried him up and left him with her, still gazing but uttering no word. When they remonstrated with him later for his silence he said: "I had no communications to make." I too have no communications to make. You don't accept my repeated and most urgent invitations to accept my more than Oriental hospitality and so won't care again to hear that my brook, swollen by recent rains, is running again. You won't care to hear how last night the whole household was disorganized by a raid made by a bat that finally came into my little library, something like yours at Pride's, and there he and I wrestled until I caught the monster resting and carried him outside. They say that they get in your hair, but I felt a certain immunity, though at times I dreaded the fate of Ganymede. You will thoroughly sympathise with us when you learn that one of our pigs has been ill, probably indigestion. Thanks to excellent local talent, a neighbour, the crisis and everything else has been passed and the little sufferer seems convalescent. . . . Don't you think it odd putting W. Churchill again into the Cabinet? What is his pull? Wasn't it enough that he blundered and kept the English army at Antwerp and so wrought its almost complete destruction? that he was mixed up in the Gallipoli business? The only thing to be said in his defense is that he doesn't seem to be mixed up in the Mesopotamian fiasco. Perhaps this is his

To John T. Morse, Jr.

reward for keeping out of that business. I haven't yet told you why I write this letter. It is because the Sabbath approaches, and do what I will, you won't go to church, and I hate to think of you with no distinct moral influences working on you from Saturday to Monday. My compliments to your lady, as G. Washington used to say. .... P. S. Monet has been commissioned to paint Rheims Cathedral as soon as the Germans get sent where they can't spoil it. He has just been down there with Clemenceau to see it. He will paint pictures which the Germans would like to destroy. Perhaps some time they will. They will go in to look at it and squirt some liquid fire on it. If the Germans shoot the American prisoners they have taken from our ship, why not confiscate some of the Kaiser's holdings in this country? He would mind that.

August 19. ... Your beautifully typed letters that kept you up all the night of the 16th and 17th reached me yesterday. Lord Charnwood has indeed come to you, if you wouldn't go to him. You can't fail to write an interesting paper. I quite agree with all you say about Andrief. You have doubtless heard me mention his name, but I have long since made up my mind that he is enormously over-rated by his admirers. I have read a lot of his stuff. I have, indeed, seen him, *vidi tantum,* on the beach at Kuokkala, and took him up under the impression that I was to read something of the greatest merit, but except in one or possibly two stories, I have been sorely disappointed. I always feel as if I were listening to a half-mad neurotic, and I really think that he must be a druggist—I mean a victim of unholy drugs. That is my diagnosis. He is a paltry soul. The one powerful story is *The Seven Who Were Hanged,* which is really memorable. It was published in English by Brentano some years ago. Phelps puts Andrief at the head of the modern men. I do nothing of the sort. There is another man, Artzibasheff, whom I rank much higher. . . . This is a heavenly day. America may be in some ways a hole, but it does have many flawless days. W. W. is still pursuing Gen. Wood. I hear that one of W. W.'s Princeton colleagues said there that if he ever took a prejudice against a man, nothing could change him. He would pursue him to the end. That's one of the reasons I call him a man too small for his job. That unamiable quality and partisanship are all the rigging a narrow man needs. . . .

August 28. . . . There seems to be a great deal of dissatisfaction with the present Ruler of the Universe. I suppose this is because he has let things get into such a dreadful state. Even the Germans, who had a deity of their own, the old German God, seem inclined to depose Him, and H. G. Wells has invented a new God of his own who is being much discussed, like every new official, by the daily press. . . .

To John T. Morse, Jr.

August 31. . . . . Here is another Friday, and our John, I am sure, wants a word of wisdom from his mentor to meditate upon in the approaching Sabbath, when he reflects on his faults and if, after that, he has any time, he makes promises of improvement. You denounced the newspapers the other day for almost avowed inaccuracy, but, my dear fellow, that is what all history is, a mere sketch built up with notoriously faulty material and dependent for its inspiration on the fancy of the time. Thus, the ballad having become an object of interest, Niebuhr writes his history to prove that Roman history was built up on a lot of lost ballads. Then see Dr. Arnold, and Macaulay's preface to his *Lays of Ancient Rome.* Mommsen rewrote Roman history to confirm his ideas of government; Ferrero to throw the light of modern politics upon it; Grote wrote his to have an argument for liberalism in his hands, etc. It is no more than what the sophists of old used to do when they made their pupils practice putting old facts into new settings. Yet, so curious is the constitution of the human mind, these changes on an old theme persuade people that they are on a steady march, or progress, to perfection. Anyone who doubts that onward movement is regarded as a vile cynic, a curmudgeon. Yet when this war is over, there may be a remission of progress, for it will take a long time to get where we were when it started. . . . The Russians seem helpless. The fact is that the peasants—the vast majority—care nothing for the war and can't see what it is waged for. Any accompanying questions of trade and government are nothing, if only they have land and can sell their crops. After all, how much would Bryan care if Boston were bombarded? He would think we were properly punished for our sins. We have had much welcome silence from him of late. . . . A heavy rain yesterday here, and my little brook is roaring like Bryan at his best. I see W. W. still favours woman suffrage, and Gerard, too. They all move that way, I suppose because they think it is coming. . . . P. S. Like a fool I forgot what I meant to say and indulged in empty and pompous declamation. I had meant to lead you slowly to the point when I should bring you up to this question, which now, without introduction, may sound a little sudden. Have you got ten thousand dollars which you would like to invest? There, I have given you a sad shock, and you imagine that I want to raise this sum for the purpose of flooding the market with the products of my farm—nothing of the sort. My aims are higher. Now you think that like C. W. E., Pius I. of his new church, Reformed Unitarian (C. W. E. is the unit and sole worshipper), I am about to introduce a new religion—no! It is to another feeling that I appeal, to patriotism. You see, I got a letter last evening, telling me that there had been raised a most graceful memorial to Com. O. H. Perry, consisting of a high colyum, which has cost more than a million dollars (I wish the money had been allotted to his needy grandchildren), that brought in $5,000.00 last year

To John T. Morse, Jr.

in fares from those lifted to its top to see if they could detect any traces of the foe that may have escaped his deadly attack. Now they find a "beautiful roomy space" in the rotunda, "just fitted for a bronze statue of Com. Perry"—a marble one would be placed on the top of the monument which, in the engraving, looks 1,000 feet high, and this statue could be placed there for no more than $10,000. Don't the family want to chip in? I am asked "for a starter in that direction." Now, as man to man, I make to you this proposition: You advance me $10,000 for this noble project, or even less. If you agree I will put up $10.00 "for a starter" and you the rest. The loan will be secured by giving you forty thousand trip tickets to the top of the monument. You can't want more than that number, and if you don't want them all yourself, you will have enough to give to friends. They will form a novel and attractive Christmas and birthday present, and will give great pleasure to the honoured recipient. . . . My sketch does no justice to the million-dollar memorial, but it will indicate the nature of the tombstone set up by a grateful nation that he saved from the horrors of subjugation. It is a pity they forget about a statue for the rotunda. I am almost ashamed to be bothering you about such a trifle, but I promise you I will gladly give, when the time comes, $20,000 for a statue (brass, bronze, marble) of any grandfather of yours that may be wanted for any rotunda. Awaiting your cheque, I am Yours, etc. . . .

Thomas Sergeant Perry

September 5. . . . I have your letter and I can't tell you how grateful I am for your generosity. I have written to the gentleman who has the financial interests of the statue in charge to tell him that you are responsible for the whole amount, and you will doubtless receive his formal thanks. Meanwhile, you have mine and those of many of the illustrious Hero's descendants. The combination of justice and generosity in your beautiful character is one of its most attractive traits. Still—how shall I say it?—you must let me call your attention to a trifling detail. I hate to mention it, but, dear and generous Sir, you or your Secretary forgot—I cannot say *neglected*— to enclose the cheque, a mere scrap of paper, but essential for business purposes. . . . Instead you sent me an amusing squib of T. R.'s talk, doubtless intended for another correspondent who must have been surprised at receiving the cheque intended for me. I only hope it was not made payable to bearer. . . .

September 9. . . . Do try again to get here and let us shake your hand. If you had come yesterday and had stayed the night, you might have heard a lecture about Germany by Joe [J. C. Grew], in the Hancock Town Hall (Hôtel de Ville), admission twenty-five cents, reserved seats, thirty-five cents. I didn't go, though everyone else did, because someone had to stay and see that the house didn't burn down. But I go to Dublin this afternoon, where it is to be

To John T. Morse, Jr.

given to that perfumed, white-gloved band of worshippers of Mammon. In Hancock it was for the French Wounded Fund's benefit.

September 26. . . . Harry Lyman, who is in the Harvey Cushing contingent in France, says he knows two things: one is that every Englishman *knows* that his side is sure to win; the other, that every German is glad to get near enough to surrender, that they have had enough and are anxious to "quit"—another word I don't like, but it says what it means. Did I tell you what M. Storey said—that from his observation, what people mean by knave is one from whom they differ on money matters; by fool, one from whom they differ on other matters. Such is his judgment after much experience. . . .

October 4. . . . I have been hearing some things about W. W. . . . It is said that no man whom he has once disliked is ever forgiven by him. He is relentless and conceives hatred of this sort for the most trivial causes. It was especially about the army and navy that my informant spoke, while giving me merely some of the lighter cases. Thus, Pershing asked at Washington for one officer of special merit, far ahead of all others in his line, but no, he couldn't go. He is to have no chance. W. W. was what he calls firm. Gen. Wood is, of course, another palpable case, but there are plenty more less known. It is a curious trait and always found in a narrow nature.

Thomas Sergeant Perry

In fact it is narrowness of the worst sort. The other side of this character is his tolerance of such weaklings as he has surrounded himself with and clings to so obstinately. A singular fate to have such a man chosen for such a post. . . . Think, too, how small the chance of getting a competent King or Kaiser. The matter is made worse for us because he is in part of our making.

Oct. 17, 1918. . . . I remember being at Emerson's at Concord shortly after I was married, when E. asked me if I knew Swinburne. I said I did not, and he told me that Longfellow, not long back from Europe, told him he had been to some great dinner at which was Swinburne, who, at the conclusion of the banquet, "sank under the table in a swound." It was the first time and the last I had ever heard the word used in talk. Emerson stood outdoors in the dim light, holding on to each elbow, while talking. . . .

Oct. 27. You may have seen that Joe Grew is gone abroad with the mysterious Col. House, and if he keeps up his diary it will be a book worth reading. Just what they are to do is very vague and, doubtless, depends on what happens. W. W., of course, wants to come out on top. I sincerely hope that his appeal for Democratic victory will be treated as it deserves. I won't begin on that man, or there'll be no stopping me. I don't suppose you read what the other Col., G. Harvey, said as quoted in Friday's *Transcript*.

To John T. Morse, Jr.

It was well worth reading. G. Harvey must feel about his introduction of W. W. to the public as the man feels who brought the gipsy moth into society, or as the still other Col. feels when he recalls his destruction of the G. O. P. Remorse seems to be the natural state of man, or if it isn't it ought to be. . . .

Oct. 28. . . . What you tell me about Lord Charnwood is rather disappointing, tho' it's just what might have been expected: the legal authorities have taken possession of him and will not let him go. That Rhodes should be unable to get a grip is indeed surprising. It must be a new experience for him. Still he will see him at the Tavern Club. I wonder if you go to their dinner. If you do you will have to make a speech, for they are still at that stage of semi-civilization at which speech-making is thought a pleasant and proper occupation. I had rather hoped to see Lord C., tho' generally I am willing to let others bask in the smile of the great, but I say to myself that I have lived over 70 years without seeing him—very contented, perhaps I can endure another 70 years without meeting him. I know at any rate that he will meet all that is really respectable in Boston. . . .

July 3, 1919. . . . Mrs. MacDowell is a most remarkable woman. There is no one like her. I have lived long under the fond delusion that my wife was no slouch when there was anything to be done, but

Thomas Sergeant Perry

by the side of Mrs. MacD. she is a mere odalisque. Mrs. MacD. got up this show [the Peterborough Festival] and runs it. For the cafeteria she brought up a *chef* from Boston and put him in charge; she commandeered beds and bedclothes from the whole countryside; she hired an orchestra of non-German players and has kept them and their instruments attuned; she herself has scrubbed floors, cleaned windows and paint, has not touched the piano for a month, and played very well yesterday afternoon; kept up her correspondence, seen thousands of people —and you know what people are—and has supervised the whole show. She has a bad back and is compelled to walk with crutches, but she gets there.[1] Here is an instance of what continually turns up at any moment. Yesterday, at rehearsal, a young woman was not present with the rest of the orchestra, but was seen in the other end of the room. Being remonstrated with, she said she couldn't play because she had met some friends and wanted to talk with them. . . . Someone managed to convey to Mrs. MacD. the state of affairs and she went forth to interview the girl. She came back in a few minutes with an air of victory and the girl played her part. Mrs. MacD. had wiped the floor with her. And of course, people being what they are, incidents like that were happening all the time. . . .

---

[1] On another occasion Mr. Perry referred to Mrs. MacDowell as "the greatest person since Napoleon." A casual estimate, which may invoke, perhaps, only a few military reservations.

To John T. Morse, Jr.

August 31. . . . I have written a stiff note to H. C. L[odge] and with the utmost difficulty have restrained myself from giving him long and minute directions for his conduct of affairs. It's strange how mighty is the tendency of human beings to tell other human beings what they ought to do and how to do it. It is almost irresistible at times. We see it in the lavishness of advice of our politicians to other nations about their problems. They need it, the politicians, sometimes, as when the N. H. delegation all voted against daylight saving, except one Senator who didn't vote at all. . . . I am not sure that college life is a certain benefit. I don't see at the Harvard Club any signs of refinement in the young men there. They speak like stable-boys and read trash. In the instruction I see some good work and much empty nonsense, or worse. I am very cross, you see, but I can't wink the facts away. It is to be remembered that whatever benefits there might be, there would be always room for criticism, as of the general ignorance of Oxford men in science, the pedantry of Germans, etc., but I am not convinced of the benefit of a college education here. . . .

Oct. 19. It is of no use for me to try to write to you, I haven't the knack. My evil nature crops out either in continual reference to your notorious faults or in venomous comments on your honourable ancestors. What the letter demands is delicate praise, what when applied to any one else I call flattery, and also fine language. To show you what I mean I enclose a beautiful model in a letter from my friend the Count de ———. I think you knew my titled friend, at any rate you will know him through and through when you have read this letter, and you will also know how a letter ought to be written and is written by a gentleman of refined culture and lofty lineage.

When in Paris last I had the distinguished honour of meeting the Count Lonejack. It was at S. Reinach's. I was not presented to him and so did not know that he had inherited the ancestral title; he rushed up to me as to a long-loved friend, and almost pressed me to his beautifully groomed bosom. What he says of his appearance is perfectly true, he looked 20 years younger than he was and was dressed like a fashion-plate. I thought he must be my only other really smart acquaintance, except Torrey [Morse] and J. F. Hyde, but we exchanged polite talk without my knowing who he was. I don't remember whether he asked me to call on him, or anything of that sort; at all events I didn't and I never saw him again. I forget how I found out who he was. I now see what I missed.

The story ran that having married a very rich wife, he persuaded her to sign a paper making over all her money to him and then separated from her, but this may be only scandalous gossip; at any rate he has no wife and has a lot of money; perhaps it came with the title. With exquisite tact when I met

To John T. Morse, Jr.

him I did not hail him with his earlier title, Brownbread, because I did not recognize him. . . .

Oct. 20. . . . Bishop told me one or two things that I have an impression I have not told you. He said that some men captured by the Germans brought back pleasanter accounts of the experience than did most. (To be sure it was near the end of the war and the Germans may have been anxious to modify the impression their brutality had produced and they wanted one friend in court.) But some of the captured aviators were treated very well and in one case he knew, the Germans having caught one man took the trouble to drop word to that effect behind the American lines. He also said that our men dropped behind the German lines statements of what their prisoners had to eat, bills-of-fare of their meals. These produced immense sensation, the hungry Germans who were captured called aloud for the promised dinner. I quite understand their state of mind. It would have been a happy thought to ring a dinner bell at intervals all along the line, from Switzerland to the North Sea, every two hours. Few Germans could have withstood the appeal; they would have flocked to the summons in a general advance of the whole army, waving their napkins instead of white flags. In the happy days of peace they used to eat a good meal about every 2 hours. Famine must have struck them with peculiar violence. . . .

Thomas Sergeant Perry

June 4, 1921. . . . On my calendar the other day was this text from Théophile Gautier: "Music is the most disagreeable and costliest of noises." I forwarded the sentiment to my musical son-in-law for his encouragement. The way to treat the artist is to kick him, to trample upon him. Only then will anything good come from him. From the crushed grape flows the choicest wine. . . .

July 14. I read Cabot Lodge's words on ½ pint of drink in 10 days as the limit of the Dr.'s power. Of course Cabot uttered incontrovertible truths, but what an extraordinary state of affairs when it should be necessary to say them. My only consolation is the ridiculous position in which those fanatics put themselves, one that should in time bring about their overthrow. Let us thank high heaven for the general decay of religious feeling in the community; with that zeal in full blast think what these fanatics might do. The Spanish Inquisition would have been a picnic by side of it. What makes fanaticism is ignorance, and there is plenty of that in this country.

There is no need of despairing because prohibition is made part of the constitution, it seems to me. There is no magic in the constitution, and it is just as easy to disregard it as to break one of the commandments. Consider all the trouble taken to give the Southern negro a vote and how they vote in fact. Northern Republicans wink at it and object to bringing up the question quite as much as the fire-eaters do.

To John T. Morse, Jr.

So in time the amendment may be no more than a mark—a high water mark—on the beach of time! Meanwhile, however, what oceans of fanaticism! . . .

June 26. . . . We were speaking ill of Mother Nature the other day, with all the harmony of a crowd of chanting angels. Listen then to a new proof of the truth of evolution, or evilution (or devilution). Did you notice the paragraph in the N. Y. *Times* the other day about the new weed in the West that has appeared and exists only to puncture automobile tires? Yes, it's like the Colorado beetle for the potato; the chestnut blighter; the boll-weevil, like all the specifics that Nature devises in her hellish laboratory for the misery of man, only this time not having been able to find an insect which it could train to eat rubber tires—she had spoiled them by pampering them with potatoes and peaches and apples—the grand inventress simply felt in another pocket where she keeps noxious weeds and tares and set this malignant devil at its task. I suppose, too, for I know the cunning intelligence at work, that the stuff clings to the tires and so spreads its seeds in every region. Soon we shall have creeping vines clambering up to the chamber windows and in, holding loaded revolvers and demanding money. That's what the future has before us. To you, O Sage, this picture will not seem too darkly painted, while the frivolous young would scorn my far-seeing prophecy, but I'm right. I always am. . . .

Thomas Sergeant Perry

July 20. Your letter has just reached me and it comes just in time to dispel a sort of blight that had fallen upon me. I had begun to fear that the incessant clack of my tongue or pen was boring you to death. I was feeling a sense of shame at my incapacity to hold my tongue and about to determine that I should never write another line in my life. It is awful to be a bore without knowing it, but a thousand times worse to be one and know it.

What you say about prohibition is most interesting. The matter is at last receiving the thought and attention that should have been given it before it was passed with such enthusiasm. In last night's *Transcript* there is a good article (contributed) on one side of the matter. The way prohibition destroys respect for the law is to me the most important thing about it and at this time most disturbing, for there is a general disposition to break down every fence. In the modern novels it is marriage that is attacked. I saw two yesterday that took up the relative merits of divorce and bigamy with decided preference for bigamy. A good many writers of verse cry for freedom, and the freedom when they get it they use like dirty little boys who write dirty little words on the fence. Certainly the parson has lost much of his old power; the politician has dug his own grave, and now law is proving itself ridiculous. With nothing to respect, anarchy is cheap. It is only a convention that one should respect the law and that convention

To John T. Morse, Jr.

is going with the rest of the lot. They will have a hell of a time when they are all gone and then they will have to set to work to rig up some new ones. . . .

July 31. . . . I am returning the Confession of Perdicaris and the 2 Blackwoods about his friend Raisuli. The 2d part about the Spanish doings in Morocco throws light on the recent battle there. The poor Spaniards are an unhappy lot, yet that despised country puts forth a lot of good work in painting, in literature and in erudition. I know a much greater country, at peace, rich, powerful, that far and away leads it in practical matters, but lingers far behind it in other respects. I think I am right, and yet we scorn the Spaniard. They showed the other day that they could play tennis pretty well, and that is a test of civilization. So is chess, and the coolies . . . of Japan play a sort of super-chess, by the side of which our game is like Old Maid compared with the most scientific whist. I seem to be defending downtrodden nations to-day, like W. W. at the conference. The resemblance between us has been often commented on by visiting statesmen and others. Our point of closest resemblance is the affection we both feel for very inferior men. There, now will you go about attacking me again? You will ask me in tortured tones when you have done so. I don't know, but the day is warm and my ink flows readily.

Thomas Sergeant Perry

Aug. 1. It was a greater convulsion of nature than I supposed. What really happened was this, the summer was blown away and autumn is firmly seated in its place. The thermometer was at 48° this morning and if we get back into our usual course without a frost we shall be lucky. It's not very far from 48° to the frostline of a still night. I am so glad we got our hay in. Many, most of our neighbours, foolish virgins, are hard at work haying. This morning M. left at 7 in her car for Boston. She has a good favoring wind, a clear sky, and, barring accident, should arrive before noon. I think she will have pleasant weather and fair breezes as far as the banks, and ought to make Boston light at abt. 11. Her fog whistle is in perfect order. . . .

My unbrilliant class has brought forth nothing of the nature of an autobiography, so far as I know, and no one has accomplished anything amazing. One of the class is now an inmate of an Old Man's Home, and I know slightly another who will probably join him if he lives long enough. Come and see me there and I will introduce you to my companions. . . .

August 11. . . . Poor Ford, knowing nothing outside of his machines, etc., is the prey of every fanatic who can get his ear. Now he believes he is doing God's work by hounding the Jews. Some of the stories he tells are ludicrously false, they have been explained a thousand times, but that makes no difference, they bob up again fresher than ever because

To John T. Morse, Jr.

they find a new generation that has never heard of them. Jews, being human, often have unlovely qualities, but if I had been persecuted, bullied, ridiculed, shunned, abused for centuries, even I might have developed some objectionable traits. The hammering they get only hardens them. I loathe Anti-Semitism and I hope I shall never forget the frequent kindness of Jews, but I detest the persecution of Jews from other than personal feelings. . . .

Sept. 1. . . . There is no need of saying anything about those damned Sinn Feiners who apparently want to go on making trouble for themselves and England and the civilized world. We don't have to go far to find barbarians. The R. C. church does not show very well in these days either in Ireland or in Boston. I was amused to see that the Pope recommends the Knights of Columbus to read Dante, for although he deserved hell fire for the way he spoke of some of the popes, it was only natural and pardonable annoyance at the harsh treatment some of his friends had received. He didn't really mean the things he said, which of course were not true; they were uttered in a Pickwickian sense. I wonder how old Dante would like being whitewashed in that way. It is my impression that he would curse and swear worse than ever. Somehow, even if the ban is lifted, I don't see large classes of the Knights going very far in Dante. I should think a decent Catholic would be sickened by the spectacle we have before us, if it were not that human nature is so elastic that we can all of us swallow anything we want to swallow and reject anything we please. Gradually by dint of living in this vale of tears I am able not to worship too blindly the events in this minute speck of the starry universe. What they wanted to get up this universe for I can't imagine. . . .

Oct. 31. . . . I see the strike does not fall. I think I was right in saying the other day that envy was one of the strongest of human passions. The French Revolution is explained as the reaction from the cruelty of the nobles. Not a bit of it. The nobles were not cruel, they were in the main very amiable creatures, and people submit to cruelty as they submit to bad weather, droughts, floods. What they can't stand is seeing other people comfortable, apparently idle, enjoying all sorts of privileges that they are denied. That makes them sick. The strikes in this country don't come about because the working people are ill treated; they are treated very well, but they see a lot of people enjoying luxury, or seeming to enjoy it, and they want a grab at it. I compress what I want to say, but you see my meaning. Of course instances of cruelty in the nobles and among manufacturers can be found as everywhere, but they prove nothing. When the railway men talk of "starvation wages", it is mere rhetoric. We all know it and they know it. No, revolution is the result of envy; we

To John T. Morse, Jr.

want the other fellow's berth and what aids this spirit is the silliness of the luxurious. . . . To go back to my favorite sin, envy, it may be said that love and hate, though doubtless ruling passions, can wait, envy can't. It is present everywhere, at all times, it is omnipresent when it exists. I think I shall propose to Lawrence L[owell] a dozen Lowell lectures on envy. I shall try them first on you, so look out! . . .

Nov. 3. . . . All I do condemn or at least smile at is setting up statues of one's own family. . . . The Belmonts to be sure put up a statue of their Com. Perry, the other one, the Jap. one, but it was a good statue, by Quincy Ward, and so should be forgiven. Fay posed for the hands. The statue of the other Commodore at Newport is most unfortunate; the hero is represented in sailor's rig, apparently dancing a hornpipe. The sculptor began life as a dentist, but soon became discontented with that miniature work. Laying aside the smaller instrument of torture, he took up the chisel, which in his hands became another, and wrought in marble. I need not say that we did not suggest the statue. Besides our invincible modesty, the costliness of sculpture stood in the way. No, a sense of shame came over Newport that the other Commodore should be exalted and their own left out and they built this image, assigning the task to native talent. I saw in a French paper last evening that Chauncey Depew put up a statue of himself and

[119]

dedicated it in a glowing oration, but I am not sure that the paper was right. Mistral saw a statue of himself put up by admiring friends, but he didn't like it. He was standing with a shawl over his arm—in the statue. He said: "There I am, going to my train, but where is my valise?" I hope I don't tactlessly cut in and dim your hope of erecting a fitting monument to S. F. B. Morse. That would be a wretched thing to do. Go to work and celebrate him, he is worthy of it. Get him done before the wireless drives the more familiar telegraph out of men's memory. Before long it will be as forgotten as the argand lamp, as the fragrance of whale oil, as the tallow dip. A good place for a statue of you would be your grass-plot. Socrates [the cat] would rest himself at the base of it. . . .

June 11, 1922. . . . Our cat is a beauty, a silver Persian with black lines in his fur. He is not a model of intelligence like Rover, for was ever a beauty anything but stupid? He is dull enough also to be very goodnatured and he seems to have no human feelings, he does not pine in the least for home and old friends. He has a purr that matches his fur, and even I can hear it. He differs from us human beings most of all in that he is goodnatured when he is hungry. He is certainly a beauty to look at and rivals suffering humanity in his swift choice of the most comfortable seat in the room; that is to say he always takes mine. . . .

To John T. Morse, Jr.

June 26. . . . Here all is as usual except that we are nearly washed off the face of the earth by what the Government calls showers but I call downpours. Saturday I went out and hoed corn like a negro slave and yesterday the rain came and crusted anew the soil I had so carefully loosened. I don't believe it does the least harm to leave it so, as God evidently meant it, but there is no convincing Margaret. . . . Are you not amused by the revolt rising everywhere against school histories? In New York, Jews, Irish, Germans are all indignant with every textbook. Some say that the English are favored; others that an Irishman hadn't credit given him, etc., etc. Prostration before the English is the most detested fault. Any hint that they were not rather worse than the modern Turks, is of the nature of treason. We are the worst winners I ever saw. We should have been worse than the Irish if they had licked us. The main difficulty that besets these critics is to find anyone capable of stating the truth in a way to please them all. I think another Constitutional Amendment must be passed requiring perfect impartiality in our historians—no favoritism for New England or Virginia but equal treatment for every colony. No defense of England. The country dependent on the Irish for everything. Anyone contradicting to be adjudged guilty of high treason. The most amusing instance is the new Confederate history in which Lincoln is accused of stealthily plotting to bring on the war. . . .

Thomas Sergeant Perry

July 5. How do you suppose our hero of the Civil War, our hardy son of 1840, passed the National Holiday? Don't be foolish, guess again, for it was not in debauchery, far from it. He determined to pay a visit to his aged sister and drove to her house and back, a distance in all of some 97 miles. He was accompanied by a lady whom you will pardon me for calling old, since her years were nearly as many as the miles she went, viz., 92. When I consider the condition of the roads and the hilly tendencies of the country, I was able to control myself when he told me she was a little tired this morning. Frank, the veteran, is not, however, and is quite able to denounce the weather with all the vigour he once manifested against the other enemies of his country. You men of 1840 are indeed a tough lot. . . . And while speaking of the stalwart veteran, I will tell you of one who was renowned for his lifelong devotion to the sex. When he had reached the age of Frank, and Wilfrid Scawen Blunt, and other great men, some one asked him if he noticed any difference that age had brought to his interest in that fascinating subject. "Yes," he answered, "I do. I find I'm not thinking of them *all* the time.". . .

September 29, 1922. . . . You, as a proprietor of poultry, can understand our feelings when M. came in yesterday morning and said that our hens, all of them, had vanished over-night. There was a to-do. We were torn in our minds as to whether some band

To John T. Morse, Jr.

of ruffians had stolen them, though it seemed impossible that even the most reckless should take so much trouble and face the penitentiary for a handful of aged, almost venerable birds. We were then more inclined, after rejecting the possibility of Indians or bears, to lay the blame to the crafty fox. Fired by this hypothesis, I at once wrote a letter to Joe, urging him to come back with the rifle that shot the tiger in distant Manchuria. I told him he could lie on the floor of the henhouse with his gun, facing the small door, and ready to shoot any object approaching, whether on two or four legs, or even on three, the number worn by a neighbouring cat. I said he would find it easier than waiting in a cave for a tiger, as he did on that memorable occasion. But what do you suppose happened? M. had gone to feed them in the morning, but there was no swift response to her call and all these lurid explanations flashed through her brain and she mourned them dead. In fact, however, they had by some accident received so much food the evening before that they left enough for a copious breakfast, and they took no interest in food and were in a comatose condition when she called. Later in the day, when I went by their late abode, I saw one strutting about and I shuddered. I thought it was the ghost of one of them and I felt exactly like Hamlet, but I knew ghosts don't eat. I wrote to Joe this morning, explaining the whole matter and begging him not to come. What a day it is! The trees are just beginning to change their colour, to moult, as we bird fanciers say. Farewell. M.'s car is out of commission with a broken chain or something. . . .

Oct. 1. . . . Such weather was never seen. I can't describe it, it is like the best of pictures. I hope, and believe, it prevails in Needham. We have our apples picked except for 5 bbls., abt. 30 in all is our humble crop. A mere crumb in your eyes, but a whole loaf in ours. Our new superintendent, as he is styled in the *Peterboro Transcript,* announcing his appointment, works well. Did I tell you that Frank, our venerable man, warmly recommended the place to him. He described us as "the goll-darndest best people he ever worked for.". . .

Oct. 2. This weather, which reminds me of the picture of the Celestial City in my grandmother's *Pilgrim's Progress,* continues. I suppose it will end with a combination of typhoon, tornado, cyclone, monsoon, hurricane, with rain, hail, snow, ice, and a temperature that shall freeze wells, rivers, oceans, may be, and find us coatless.—You see I know the ways of nature.—That last night I was at your house, at least the afternoon before, there was a tornado at Antrim, 4 or 5 miles from here, that almost flattened our granite hills. It threw down barns, knocked down trees, went through the whole performance. . . .

Oct. 3. . . . Superintendent is a far more impressive title. It suggests an estate, with granite posts,

To John T. Morse, Jr.

and huge barns, and various splendours not to be found here. I wish, however, that I had offered you the job and that you had undertaken it. You would have found me a stern but invariably just taskmaster. Outside of your working hours you would have found me affable and almost chatty. In our altered positions you would not have found me so ready to listen, and you would have learned that art yourself, difficult as you would have found it! You would have found me glad to instruct you in the rudiments of agriculture. Indeed, I might have done you much good in many ways, and at the end you would have echoed the diluted profanity of Frank when he placed us high among the goll-darndest.

It is now Oct. 4, and what a day it is, cool but seasonable. If it were not for this accursed odour of burning wood I should be happy, but it is impossible to determine if the blaze is in Wisconsin or just the other side of the mountain, preparing to drive us refugeeing to the village. The leaves seem to change from hour to hour, and when we can photograph colours directly, it will be amusing to take the same view at brief intervals to see the rate of change. And as the leaves fall the trees come into view, as even you may have noticed. . . .

October 23. . . . That frost the other night (18° and lower outside) caught the leaves on many of the trees and simply froze them while yet green. Thus a gingko, a cherry and a pear tree close to the house. I never saw this before. . . . M. had about $20.00 worth of celery hit. She thought at first it was a total loss, but it is not so bad as that. Under Providence it owes its escape to the fact that it was enwrapt —a great part of it at least—by loving hands in copies of the N. Y. *Times* of recent date. This is an excellent paper with many good qualities, which gives us all the news that is fit to print and some that isn't, as for example some of the details of the tragedy that has cast a shadow on New Brunswick, N. J., and the Episcopalian Church. The impression made on my mind is so deep that I am about to send to my N. H. Senator an earnest request that they prepare a bill pointing out once more how much trouble and confusion the existence of women causes in an otherwise happy world; how they rend families apart, spread misery by leading young and old into temptation, luring them to ruin, etc., etc. A ghastly picture of the harm they have done and are doing, could be painted by any advocate who had read even moderately. I then suggest the 20th amendment to the constitution that shall order the prohibition of women within the borders of the U. S. and its dependencies, their introduction into this country or their existence here, save and except only such as have been acquired before the passage of this amendment. The jurisdiction of this country extending to 3 miles from shore, any women crossing that limit shall be thrown overboard. Of course the details will be worked out by the Senators' secretaries, but it will be a happy day

To John T. Morse, Jr.

when that shall become the law of the land and we shall be free of another source of misery and woe. So shall the names of Volstead and Perry go ringing down the centuries as the great deliverers of humanity, freeing it from the two curses that have embittered it from the remotest date. Eve was, alas! in the garden of Eden and Noah evidently was a moonshiner. Mr. Morse, will you join me in this noble work? I will let you have some of the glory. We need financing and those cheques which didn't go to pampering the Republican party would come in very handy here in these dark days of taxpaying. A word is enough. You have my address.

Nov. 11. These are eventful days. The poultry house is growing like Jonah's gourd, like a palace in fairyland, and yesterday, a day too soon, the man brought from Antrim 36 pullets. What shall be done with them? They can't be left loose in a house of which only the ribs are up. That would be as rash as to sail in a similarly emaciated boat. Are they to be brought into the house? How about the studio? or Alice's? or the periscope?[1] All these suggestions flashed through my mind, but there was no occasion for distress, all was arranged for by M. The icehouse, now empty, had been made over for a residence of cockerels, and needed only a few touches to be ready for the 36 strangers who entered, partook of a luxurious meal and tho' they laid 14 eggs in their

[1] "Perryscope." A portable house, so named by Moorfield Storey.

Thomas Sergeant Perry

Antrim home yesterday, laid 2 this morning after all the exciting and distracting novelties of their first trip from home. Meanwhile I am reminded of the war-time energy of the Shipping Board by the fury with which the Industrial Home is built. There we hope they will pass their first Sabbath in Hancock and many happy years. On the arrival of these little strangers I was moved to make them a speech, or rather an address, which I wish you had heard. I won't write it all out for you. It is too long, but if it is printed in the Peterboro' *Transcript* I will send you a copy. I began: "Hens, I welcome you as sisters, for like you (they are R. I. Reds of the purest blood) I come from Rhode Island. In this bleak climate I recall, as you do, the balmy zephyrs that temper excessive heat and moderate the cold. You must feel at home with me." Then I went on: "You will soon see in golden letters over [1] the door of the palace which we are preparing for you, the name of one of the greatest friends of your noble race that the world has ever seen. The raising of your race from neglect, from partial obscurity, has been the highest aim of his life. At times he has relaxed, with a brain wearied by solicitude for you, into writing books and obituaries, (These he does with marvellous skill. I will read you some, one of these days. I say nothing about the books), but his real interest is the feathered

---

[1] "J. T. Morse Jr. Industrial Home for Hens" was Mr. Perry's suggestion after receiving Mr. Morse's beautifully drawn plans.

To John T. Morse, Jr.

race of the farmyard. He has studied how best to house you, and that he has succeeded you will perceive when you enter your new home. His devotion to you and yours has been rewarded with great wealth and many honours, and were he proud, he could dazzle your eyes with ribbons and medals testifying to his prowess."—The peroration or Perry ovation was simply magnificent, when I made an appeal to their better nature, bade them to turn a deaf ear to all bolshevik agitators, and to show "that the R. I. red was not the Moscovite red." They seemed much touched and it was very soon that those eggs were laid. I almost wish you could have heard my remarks, though my lavish praise of you would certainly have embarrassed you, but you would have liked it.—My own active brain has been at work, and L.'s too. She wanted the two eggs left in the nest that they might show the hens an aim in life, but M. said, No! I propose painting the walls of the palace with countless pictures of eggs. Did you ever try that? Let me know how it worked. . . . The trouble with being progressive and trying to introduce new things (is) that one dabbles with all the old theories that have been proved worthless by ruinous experience. What would be new would be the application of wisdom. Really I think the society of poultry is more agreeable than that of our congressmen. I now understand your preferring them to American Statesmen. . . .

Thomas Sergeant Perry

June 17, 1924. . . . Your letter crossed my humble scrawl and has proved of the greatest service in showing that there was someone with a proper appreciation of the nominal head of this household. What you say of the inferiority of American writers is painfully true, and you would feel it only more acutely if you were condemned to read some of the literary journals and magazines of this unhappy country. What is most apparent is a sort of flippancy that reminds one of the talk of the man of the world who is for the moment managing a circus, when he chats with the clown. The Senate has hardly fallen lower than most of the writers. In both we see the same enthusiasm for Democracy and the same envious hatred of anything like dignity. . . . Another glorious thing is that [our] tall clock, my grandfather's clock, after long silence, has begun to go. It suddenly struck one day, and then refused to strike or even "to march." I tried everything, moved it a bit, sought the perfect level, spoke to it words of encouragement, of reproof, but nothing would do and I was heart-broken; for Mr. Hanson (who still cuts the hair of Hancock swells who are above having their hair cut by their wives and would be glad to take the place of Schreider when you are here, terms moderate, and no tip) refused to come and look at the clock. But yesterday I started it in despair and now it goes. I am rash in thus bragging of it for I know I am tempting Providence, and how miserably incompetent Providence is to resist a temptation. One

To John T. Morse, Jr.

would think that instead of his creating us we had created him. Perhaps we have. . . .

June 23. . . . My flower garden (our Mr. Perry gives his attention to pansies exclusively) grows apace and I have a radio! Joe made me a present of one. It is not installed and I don't quite know where we can put it, for all the space in the barn is needed for hay for the three cows who supply our *customers,* and the radio itself promises to be about as large as the old Music Hall organ. It is, as I told Joe, like going to a Red Indian's wigwam and proposing to the savage to instal a telephone. Yet there are little boys in the village who have a perfect understanding of this miraculous thing, parts of which look like fireless cookers, flatiron heaters, etc. Then there is a switchboard. When you have learned to manage this intelligently, everything is simple. Thus you set the key (called the annunciator) at W.J.B. and at once you can listen to Mr. Bryan telling a bedside story, making a speech, or singing a comic song—or hymn, as you prefer. . . . I really know nothing about the radio, and in thunder storms I am in a twitter lest the electric fluid should magnify and do great harm. It will be agreeable to be able to find out at any moment the exact time, for I hate to interrupt Mr. Brown at the station with a question that may seem to him insignificant. I have a fear that many of the winged words that come through the radio may not be so interesting. Nothing could make me go to hear a speech, not so much because I dislike going as that I abhor hearing one, and when I have sought and found silence among the eternal hills, there is something dreadful about the thought that if I turn whatever you turn and put clappers on your ears you will hear Mr. McAdoo braying, or Pat Harrison, or anybody. It's curious and shows how the world moves. . . . I know all our words and actions are wandering about in space to be heard and seen of man when this thing is a little improved, and he will sometime turn on T. S. P. I hope this will be after my death. I couldn't stand the revelations. I desire no rehearsals of the Day of Judgment. I will now end as sermons used to end when I had to sit under them. Let us all try so to live that we may not fear what any kind of a radio may say about us. . . .

July 2. . . . Your Sabbath Day message reached me in due course, and it seemed full of the spirit of that blessed festival and inspired by the quiet of the country. It bespoke a nature in harmony with itself and its surroundings, critical to be sure of the evil done by sinners, yet hopeful of a peaceful end. . . . Here all goes on as of yore. We, too, are haying, cutting not so glorious a crop as yours in the subtropics, but such sparse tufts as can painfully grow on our sandy, gravelly desert. We have made large purchases of whole prairies for the sustenance of our kine and horses. The coyness of the sun is vexatious,

To John T. Morse, Jr.

but when is the farmer happy? I will not sing our woes lest you should start up and sing your own, which are infinitely less interesting. Ours would inspire Homer to a third song. You will have noticed the state of mind of Japan with regard to this country. The scorn of the veiled threat was of course magnificent, but is it good statesmanship to make the Government hated by everyone? We do our best to make ourselves odious to the English, to the French, to the Japanese and to fill with hatred ten million negroes at home. Is it worth while? It seems to me that there are practical objections to absolute cubbishness as a rule of life, but it is the prevailing sentiment that it is the essence of manliness. There! You see that though it isn't Sunday, I can howl and wail over all things just as well as you can. I *am* a pessimist, a professional pessimist, and so am universally respected. I expect in time to receive a degree from some college of P.D., Dr. of Pessimism. My oration on that occasion will be magnificent, and after it nine-tenths of the hearers will go out and hang themselves. . . .

July 4. . . . Old garlic is like an old beet, an old potato, only worse, but the new, fresh from heaven might have been the most delicious ornament of Paradise before Adam's fall. In proof of this statement, let me tell you that once when L. and I had bicycled to Brescia, and after looking at pictures were sitting outside of a café at our mid-day meal, she said: "This is a most delicious omelette, what is the delicate flavour?" I tasted it and told her it was the detested, denounced garlic. Oh, human injustice! It is all of a piece, with the hounding of Jews, of Japanese, of negroes, this condemnation of one of the world's great wonders. You know the delicate palate of the lady whose unsolicited tribute I have quoted. You know how almost the only things she can eat are plain (but carefully boiled, twenty minutes, etc. rice) and bread and butter. Even rice pudding is too rich for her, and for her to choose garlic for praise puts a new light on things. I wish I had an acre of it. You didn't read Bryan's speech in praise of McAdoo, I'm sure, but I did and got much fun from it. It was amusing to see how they heckled him and how angry he got, for he is more accustomed to lavish praise. The talk of some of those men is the most idiotic I think I have ever seen. What is equally idiotic is surprise at seeing it. It is with that grist that the world is run. Fortunately in a certain number of years the gasoline supply will have dried up, all the coal will have been dug, all lakes, rivers and water sources will have vanished, and then the human race will become extinct. It will be a better world then. . . .

July 5. . . . There were little things I meant to say, but they got crowded out. One was that my rosy picture of the end of the world was probably false, because perhaps—if the people didn't do as they have

To John T. Morse, Jr.

done in Russia and annihilate the intelligentsia—they would discover unknown ways of keeping warm, such as extracting and preserving the latent heat of icebergs. There would be nothing stranger in that than in drawing from the eternal silence of the heavens the equally eternal jaw-work of W. J. Bryan. . . .

July 11. . . . I had also thought of confiding to you, very privately, some hint of the approaching revolution which is to shake Hancock to its foundations. Yes, the intelligentsia was, perhaps is, about to rise against the vile capitalist monopoly that seized the milk business here. There has been a good deal of murmuring of late among the populace. Scraps of their eloquence have reached my ears. I told L. that I now understood why rich people in Dublin kept no cows: they wanted a chance to taste cream once in a while. I denounced the alleged cream put before me: "Is there no way of distinguishing from skim milk except by putting some in a large, some in a small jug?" Sophists said, "the calf takes it all." I answered: "The Golden Calf?" I pointed out that we got no more milk from our three cows than from the Milky Way. I said that if any man ever invited me to his dairy farm and told me what a lot of cows he had, and all in the social register, I should thank him and tell him I should be delighted to come over Sunday and will bring a tin of evaporated cream with me. "I wish you would bring two while you are about it. I like cream in my coffee." One consequence of these delicate hints that rumbled around here, like thunder in the mountains, had a good result, and this morning there was a little cream. . . . Last evening the magician came to put our radio together and there it is in the dining room, looking like some pagan shrine, and as if it might be covered with runic inscriptions. Still it does not work. L. asked me, when our hopes were highest, what the choice was for the evening's entertainment. I picked out a talk in Omaha between the Rev. Mr. Brown and Mr. Smith, but we were disappointed, "nothing doing"; this new idol was as silent as the statue of Memnon. I told L. that perhaps if it got going some screw might slip so that we couldn't stop it and bedtime would come but no one could sleep on account of the hot discussion between Rev. Brown and Smith, so that we should have to telegraph to Omaha to get someone to tear the men apart. In fact, I don't believe there is anything in it at all. It is all a mass of unfulfilled promises. It advertises well and then excuses itself. . . .

July 13. . . . I have, for a long time, been painfully aware of the indifference, the dislike, even sometimes the repulsion that I arouse in those into whose society I force myself. I need give no particulars, the fact is there, but at least I have found a way out. I have learned the secret of popularity, a sure way of winning the interest, perhaps the affec-

To John T. Morse, Jr.

tion, of lovely women, lots of them. It is to commit murder and be condemned. That is all I need. The cutting I send along will illustrate what I mean. . . . Observe the defense of Muir. First he shot to intimidate his foe, second, he was so drunk he could have no evil intention. Why are murderers so fascinating to women? They have a contempt for all other men, but murderers inspire only admiration. Why do people like to put on uniforms, however absurd, and march together in mid-July, in baking streets? I can understand and sympathize with almost any murderer, but I do not understand the Elk or any of the marching Fauna. Yet there must be a strong connecting tie that brings the men together. . . .

July 20. . . . I agree with your Thackeray eulogy, but why on that account hate Dickens? D. was, it is true, rank with vulgarity, but still a genius. I was amused at seeing in a diary I have been reading, or some magazine, that a man said: "It's odd, whenever I get into a police court, it is crowded with Dickens characters." I like green peas, must I then "score" tomatoes? The epicure likes everything good. . . .

July 27. I wish I knew your address. Does the mere mention of Needham suffice? I feel the uncertainty that one might have, if such correspondence were lawful, about the writing to one newly dead. Out of politeness one wouldn't want, however convinced of its accuracy, to put down in black and white, J. T. M., Jr., Esq., Hell, and there would be great danger of its getting lost if it were sent to Heaven—"no such person here", and it might be that you meanwhile were in Purgatory, but politeness required sending to Heaven first. Only the rude and tactless would add: "Please forward." I can't write without having the aim of the letter in my mind, any more than I can open the door of an empty room and fling into it a wise or even intelligible remark; so if you don't get this letter, no harm is done. Another reason for gloom is that it has been decided that we don't spend next winter in town. L.'s health requires a softer clime, and we shall go to Washington and then further south, to horrid drafty hotels, overheated, smelly, noisy, loathsome. Nothing to read, nothing to see, enforced meetings with odious fellow-beings—it's awful! I shall never smile again, and probably shall never live at 312 again. I had better sell my books and the house. Expect no more letters from me, my spirit is broken and one can't spread one's groans about. It isn't nice, so I stop doing it.

August 1. . . . I had some talk the other day with a man who winds through the country between here and Boston in behalf of electric lights, and I asked him what he picked up in the way of politics. He told me that he finds great interest in the K.K.K., more than I should expect, and that many will quietly abstain from voting for any man who denounces it.

To John T. Morse, Jr.

The fact is that the more degraded religious (so-called) sects of America are suffering from swollen heads and desire to control everything. They are just like the Inquisition. They want to control education, to suppress the teaching of evolution, to degrade the whole people to their level of ignorance and bigotry. It must amuse the R. C.'s to find themselves charged with heresy. They must feel like the English who, travelling on the continent, said: "We are not foreigners, we are English." I yearn for the long reign of a despot who will not bother us with elections every four years, especially when the years are so short as they are nowadays. It is hardly worth while for the entering President to unpack his trunk in the White House, for he will have to put his things back in it at once. Yes, democracy is a glorious thing when everyone is wise, just as Communism is when all are generous. In fact, when human beings are faultless, they will be governed very easily. The ruler will only have to come out every morning and bow to his people, who will salute him with affability and reverence, and his day's work will be done. While, however, human nature is prone to sin, the question of government cannot be solved, any more than we can settle by law which side we shall lie on in bed. . . . It is bitterly cold here. I suppose local pride prevented your seeing that the other day Boston (95°) was hotter than New York (91°), Philadelphia (94°) and Washington (94°). Yes, Boston über alles. Our cow soon revived and is now well again. Her recovery was as swift as her breakdown. The man was up with her about all night, dosing and treating her with this happy result. I confess I despaired, but then I always despair. Then, it was in some such feeling that I began this letter and I have very nearly brought it to an end. I have got through the letter, but I despair of the Republic....

August 5. . . . In a few days there is to come over a Mrs. Cohen, who has greatly taken L.'s fancy. She is a Russian Jewess, who came to this country when very young, lived in the East side of New York, worked in sweatshops and gradually managed to educate herself and to emerge. The story, and it is a most interesting one, is told in *Out of the Shadows,* by Rose Cohen, New York, 1918. . . . It's worth reading to see what people can do. You will notice that her education bears very little resemblance to that of Henry Adams, but it gave its owner much more satisfaction. I have not seen the lady who, I am told, looks like a child. I sent her over yesterday by L. a Russian book that I thought might interest her, but she sent it back because she can't read Russian! She left that country at, say ten, and hadn't learned to read—they were all peasants—and in this country had enough to do learning English. She has learned it well and writes stories in the *Pictorial Review* (a sort of underclothes magazine with an immense circulation) that pays her vast sums for each one. I have read two of them, about peasant

To John T. Morse, Jr.

life in the old country. They are good. I am curious to see her. . . . I have been out to see my cats play, yes *cats,* for we have been adopted by a yellow and white Tom-cat with double paws and a head as large as that of a hippopotamus. He is no beauty but he is impressive. Our hearts are wrung with anxiety as to what we shall do with him this winter. We can't leave him to die of hunger here, perhaps we'll make a present of him to you!

August 9. . . . Mrs. Cohen came over and was most agreeable. You must see her book when you come. It tells the story of her life as a young girl in the East side of New York, working hard. She has a daughter eighteen years old and looks about that age herself. We hope to get her over again and you must see her. She would greatly interest you both. She is a remarkable creature, and very charming as well as sincere. . . .

October 24. . . . Yesterday I came across a very acute French phrase, which applies to a great many political leaders: *"Il attendait l'impossible, et c'est l'inévitable qui l'a atteint."* (Not an easy sentence to translate into equally neat form). Don't you think it capital? I go about repeating it to myself as if I were hurling it in the face of Lenin, LaFollette, Pussy Foot, and other demagogues. . . . You won't do it, so I need not recommend you to read Marcosson's paper on Russia in this week's *Saturday*

Thomas Sergeant Perry

Evening Post. Marcosson is a very able fellow and very honest, and his tale is impressive. He has interviewed all the Bolshevik leaders and put down what they say—perhaps the inevitable will hit them—it's very interesting. It's a blessing that the great American people have so much material offered them for making up their minds about current questions. I must say, too, that I read with the keenest interest Jim Corbett's story of his active youth. It's very well told and of course of wide interest. What an aristocracy we have in this country, a close body of billionaires. They are our real nobility, and just as France suffered from a nobility that had rights but no duties, so this country suffers from the dreariness of the outlook for the sons of our nobles. They inherit possibly capacity, certainly position, and what is there for them to do? No wonder their principal occupation is deserving and securing divorce. All they accomplish is making the display of wealth odious but desirable in the eyes of others. Do not be alarmed, I stop here. . . .

Ponkapoag, May 14, 1925. Venerable Sir: . . . My mind is like the desert, the great American desert I call it. I have done nothing, seen nothing. Oh! I did see on George Agassiz's bookshelves Harvey Cushings's very new life of Osler, two big, thick volumes. . . . That is what a busy man does. He gets up early, rushes to the hospital and performs exhausting work there for some hours, sees private

To John T. Morse, Jr.

patients all the rest of the day and at night, when he ought to be sleeping, writes an intelligent book. You have only to look at the book to wonder how a man can put it together, and always only a secondary thing. If I were going to write a life like that I should have Marlborough St. covered with straw; I should petition Mayor Curley to divert all traffic; I should ask Bishop Lawrence for special prayers at the Cathedral; should never find time to look at a paper—but he turns it off without a murmur. Another book I saw there was my old friend the *Pirate's Own Book*. On that and the *Mariner's Chronicle* I was brought up. They are delightful books, as full of blood-curdling tales as the morning newspapers. . . .

May 25. . . . It is odd to notice how strong is the notion of the present age that everything can be settled by a legislature. Man is to be made temperate by passing a law; evolution is destroyed in the same way—but all these wise thoughts will suggest themselves to even your intelligence. We shall have to do something to make the world safe from democracy. In fact we want to make the world safe from thinking that any word is going to do anything, or at least everything. This whole row seems to me immensely interesting, not only because it brings back the old Inquisition—and on both sides, for some of the conservative excesses are incredible . . . some of the actions against free speech are abominably absurd. When a man wants to have some gunpowder burnt, he doesn't put it in a box and sit on it. He sets fire to it in the open air. On the other hand, I see no immediate limit to the demands of the vast, ignorant, arrogant voting public, bent on bringing everything down to their level. We see ignorance adopting all the forms of civilization as we see Moroccans using airplanes and machine guns. As for Bryan, what a name he will leave behind him. He is sure of immortality, which ever side wins. Really, the longer I live, the more this world puzzles me. If it comes to taking sides I should think it more nobly democratic to belong to a family building up from lowly, even simian origin, than to one of immense downfall from a god-like origin. I am going now to look for a roomy, well-ventilated cave, with a Southern exposure, for the time when all civilization is destroyed. . . .

May 27. . . . Yesterday, feeling my youth renewed, I snatched up my spud and rushed forth to battle with the dandelions. That is really my sole agri ⎱ horti ⎰ cultural interest. Ploughing, harrowing, sowing, cultivating, hoeing, weeding in any form, harvesting in any shape, are joys that soon bring with them complete satiety. Gypsy and other moths, beetles in any shape, cut and all malevolent worms, San José scale, pests of all descriptions I hate and loathe, but I bow before them. They never touch my goat (if I may use the language of the streets out here in the coun-

To John T. Morse, Jr.

try) but a dandelion is like the sight of a glass of wine to Charles Eliot since he reformed, or that of an orphan asylum to a German army in war-time; it is something to be annihilated. If it were not for the infernal fecundity of the horrid weed I should long since have made it as rare as flower lovers have made the Cardinal flower, but it's a fight for us both. I am armed with a deadly weapon in the shape of a thick walking stick, with a sharp nail that penetrates the weed and then exudes a cobra-like poison. I have long since discarded the kitchen knife, which demands constant bending and bowing, both undignified, and have substituted the spud, a variation, as the name implies, of the spade. Mr. Edison and I are in correspondence about some of the details of a simple invention of mine, harnessing the electric fluid and discharging it into the vitals of the weed and destroying it. The ladies of Hillsborough Co. were about to take action against me for cruelty towards one of the most beautiful objects in nature, leaving them to languish by the wayside. In fact, I was cruelly misrepresented, for I tried that once but nature got ahead of me and when I wasn't looking, turned the flowers into airy, feather-like things that spread contagion everywhere and the last state of my noble lawn was worse than the first. Now I am wiser, and either burn the pesky weed when the ladies of Hillsborough Co. aren't looking, or—I will now tell you a great secret and let you into a sure thing, to wealth beyond the dreams of avarice—feed them to the hens. That's my discovery, or rather, that of my new man who told me yesterday—and I tried it, and it's true; the hens ate them greedily. Now, my plan is this: we pick, or better, have picked, a lot of dandelions, grind them up to a convenient size, put them into what some people call cartons, and others, paper boxes. These we label—see how generous I am—*"Morse's* Spring Tonic for Heavy-Hearted Hens." There will be on the box the reproduction of a photograph of you wearing all your poultry and hen medals. I will send a letter to the papers about meeting Old Man Morse, the famous poultry fancier, of Norfolk Co., whose birds are, etc., etc. I can do it. Sir, our fortune is made. The composition of our tonic—and a tonic in the form of a powder, is already a wonderful advance—had best be kept a secret. I think the discovery rivals Texas oil wells in "potential" wealth. The well-known bitterness of the weed, herb rather, cannot fail to improve the appetite of the bird and its example may augment its fertility. In time we may find it beneficial for suffering humanity. In old days, when I was dining with Sam Ward at the Commonwealth and you were growling outside, yearning to throw a stone through the window, that arbiter of elegance used to drink dandelion coffee while I absorbed, in aristocratic ease, the more savory juice of Mocha and Mecca. Think for a moment of the fortune made from simple celery and think what we could do with my new discovery.—Mr. Morse, are you with me in

To John T. Morse, Jr.

this affair? I let you in not on the ground floor, not in the cellar, but on bedrock. A prompt letter with a cheque proportionate to our enthusiasm will be most welcome for a few primary expenses. Perhaps Miss S. would like to sell her place and go in with us. Anxiously awaiting your reply, I am, Sir, Yours always. . . .

May 29. . . . But, as I was going to say, what I call my conscience reminds me that I must make my apologies for a lie I told you the other day. The new heifer is not to be in the Herd Book. I misunderstood Margaret. The mistake was the result of my infirmity. I don't hear half that is said, and nature, which seeks to compensate for every loss, makes me hear lots of things that are not said. Balancing the account at the end of the year, I don't find that it makes much difference. Nature does her best with that infinite care which we all admire. She is never tired of these good actions, as for example, when she has been pestering a man for a long time with rheumatism in his right hand, she relents, takes it away and puts it carefully in his left hand. . . . When you consider how much she has to do, in so many universes that we know about from reading the magazines, and doubtless as many more that we know nothing about, it is not strange that a little thing like that should escape her attention, though I am more observant. M. then did not say what I said she said. The poor heifer has no position in the social world.

Thomas Sergeant Perry

She is an outcast. I don't think she is yet aware of this stain, but I can't be sure. Her mother should have been entered in that Golden Book, but was not, and the portals of Heaven were closed. I believe five grades (one more than the four quarterings required in Austria and elsewhere) will open them. The day is agreeably warm at last. It's a novel sensation. The day I last saw you the thermometer in town reached 83°! . . . You ought to see my pansies; they don't mind the cold. They are huge, almost as large as sunflowers. I love them of any size. They are modest, and have a complicated expression, puzzling, like the cat's, which they resemble. . . . At this point I stem the eager current of thoughts and write your address on the envelope. I hope you don't notice of what an unfashionable shape the envelope is, and I have laid in a lot of them. I bought them on a falling market. I began to use them about forty years ago when I was corresponding with Addington Symonds. I sent him my letters in those parallelograms that we pay our bills in—when we pay them—and he, like a real gentleman, sent his brilliant replies in square enclosures. At last, when I had irretrievably stained my reputation, I bought the kind you may see about this letter. Now, all self-respecting people use an envelope shaped between this and the bill-payer, with a huge flap like a cow's tongue. Anything else is wrong. Anyone using the kind I palm off on an old-timer like you, is what the late Barrett Wendell called B. Franklin, "not technically a gentleman."

To John T. Morse, Jr.

. . . Doesn't it seem to you the most absurd thing in the world that anyone, even a politician, should want to put the law on the men who talked about the French debt in Paris? So far as I know, they expressed an opinion held by a great many people, that we should go easy with that debt. Since when is that a crime? The next step will be imprisoning Democratic senators for speaking against Republican bills. (It might be a good thing to do.) If things go on in this way, we shall spend our declining years in Fort Warren or on Deer Island. I propose starting a revolution. . . .

May 30. . . . I am sending you the June *Harper's,* to which I have subscribed, to have something adapted to the inferior intellect of my lady. When my more powerful brain, after the exhausting labour of writing a suitable letter to you, at last craves refreshment, next I take up the magazine myself and I think that you, shattered by disease, suffering, dissipation, may like to look at it. . . . The man who writes about Dickens says some things worth hearing, but how he does hate the nineteenth century! The widespread denunciation of that very respectable period enlivens many contemporary articles, and this man Boyd is in the middle of the mob. He wrote an article on Milton the other day and flew at him with some violence because the nineteenth century had admired him. One would have thought that Milton's views on divorce would have held his hand for a moment, but no. I dare say we deserve it all, and I am sure they deserve all they will get from their grandchildren. I am reminded of the certainty of every class entering college that it was the best class ever. Traces of that boyish enthusiasm still cling to the remnants of the class of '60—at least so I am told. . . . I have been looking at a book by Perry Belmont, which he gave to L. last winter, when she was in Washington. Its aim is to show that America has never been isolated from Europe, etc. Is he right in saying that the notion that—I'll copy the whole paragraph: "The writer was a member of the history class of Prof. H. Adams at Harvard. Some of the contributors to what is known as the American Statesmen Series, a useful historical work, founded by H. A., were selected from that class," at page 53. Page 54 goes on: "John T. Morse, Jr., was selected by Mr. Adams as the editor of the series." Does your blood boil? Above all things, be calm. You must now have a relapse. Whatever you may decide to do, there must be no duel. It is in his blood, *our* blood. His father was wounded in a duel; Com. Perry fought, I believe, two in his short (but brilliant) life. No, you would have no chance if you should be so unhappy as to stand facing the bore of a pistol held by one of us. You would find it an awful bore, for we shoot to kill. Be warned in time, and let the matter be arranged quietly, privately, by some discreet friend of both parties. I shall be very willing to lay aside everything and to take the part of adjudi-

To John T. Morse, Jr.

cator myself. How discreet I am this letter shows already. It is not for me to dwell further on my excellence in that respect. I think I can arrange matters without scandal. You may be calm. No one will read the book. His thesis is an unpopular one. . . .

June 1. . . . I am alone. My family has deserted me. This morning they started off at an early hour and are now probably well on their way to Reno. It was the the old story: incompatibility. I am brave —I utter no moans. . . . I have nothing else to record and I have nothing else to slip into the envelope to make you forget the emptiness of my poor brain. I do want to chat about the proposal to "stabilize" the franc at its present value, 25 centimes. I don't see how it can be done, and I don't see how it can be avoided. It has been done elsewhere, and so can be done with France. I suppose the leaders will arouse enthusiasm by saying the change soaks the rich, whereas in fact it will hit everyone. It will be well, if it is to be done, that the change should take place under a radical government. It must be done, it seems to me. The new franc will be like the old Spanish real that prevailed in Spain when I was there for the first time. It was about five centimes, and it gave us the impression, by the huge total of the bills, of possessing, but having to expend, colossal fortunes every time we spent a week in a hotel. If you at all follow French politics, you must occasionally be amused. The interest of the communists in the Riffian republic outdoes ours in that of the Philippines. In Saturday's *Transcript* there is a notice of a book by a woman named Mayo on those distracted islands, which seems to let in a good deal of light on the question. There is a good deal of nonsense talked in this world, and the statement that men are and should be free and equal is the most enormous misstatement. Lots of men would be better under control, and as to equality, one might as well say all trees grow to the same height. But we all love to have our thinking done for us, like the modern breakfast supplies. Really, some things are too absurd. Yet if they weren't absurd, they wouldn't be human. Could there be anything more absurd than my making a fuss about this, the inevitable and perpetual conduct of the human race? Is my discovery so great after all? Have I stumbled on a novelty?—I won't go on. I have written enough to show just why my family left me. They simply couldn't stand any more of my talk, and they will only have to show this letter to any Judge to have him grant the divorce at once. . . .

June 4. . . . You know how in every village there is one matchless orator, the pet of his family, who goes down to the station twice a day to see the train go by, and then to the village store to say what Coolidge, what Baldwin, what Painlevé, what Hindenburg ought to do and what he would do if fate

To John T. Morse, Jr.

had placed him in some such position. You know how nothing is good enough for him, how those presidents and ministers do their best to please him, but always fail; you know his high ideals, you know the man I mean. Well, I am one of that race. I am the village growler. . . .

June 10. . . . I have been having a good deal of fun. I have got hold of a novel, *South Wind,* by the old Calabrian, i.e., Norman Douglas, the man who wrote *Old Calabria,* a book I raved about last year. Some unknown person—human being or divine, I can't tell which—left it here. This novel has the same charm, it might have been written by a faun, one more intelligent than most of the race and one more full of learning. It is "replete" with the most delicious irony, and a flavour of cynicism runs through it like the corrective bitter in a well-formed cocktail. It is not devoid of malice, and malice, properly administered, gives charm to a book as it does to life. I find as I read the book that I feel once more what I call a wise smile, i.e., a certain twitching of seldom used muscles in my upper lip, that I have hardly felt since I read Jules Le Maître. He is certainly very amusing. One can't read too much at a time, any more than one can live on one dish, but I enjoy it mightily. You would agree with many of the words the wiser characters utter. They sound, when I read them, as if they were falling from your lips, and than that I know no higher praise. L. has not read it yet, and I fear she wouldn't like it. The writer's moral sense is not his strong point; he knows the world too well. I think few women would care for the book. They would be only pained by it, but you would like it; at least I do, and you know I am not prejudiced in favour of novels.. . . . It is but faintly indecorous; it is the view of life, the paganism, that women would hate. . . .

June 23. . . . The *Wall Street Journal* always interests me, as you know. In a world that is so full of emptiness it is delightful to hear one voice speaking so wisely and so clearly and so briefly. There are no shavings, no superfluous words. Sometimes, to be sure, it is only the superfluous words that people like. They call them eloquence. I think the last bit of eloquence I heard was in a speech of the modern Demosthenes, Gov. Rice, uttered, delivered, pronounced at a commencement about fifty years ago, when I was young and green and went to commencements. He spoke of ships and called them "the white wings of commerce." I knew at the time that it was my last look at a precious gem once common but soon to disappear, and it has disappeared. The only survival is in those epitaphs applied to recipients of degrees at Cambridge, which arouse such unbecoming wrath in me every June. They always sound to me as if they had been composed in Latin and then translated by some blundering freshman. At Yale they

To John T. Morse, Jr.

have a much more familiar and homelike address; this I prefer to our pomp. . . .

July 21. Here I am forgetting all my civilities and I ought to acknowledge your letter from Boston. I am very sorry they have put on your shoulders the composition of the letter about Mr. ——. It is a great mistake to be amiable and to spread abroad the impression that one is considerate and kind to others. It is a vice that brings swift and bitter punishment. Thank Heaven, though my sins are many, that one I have avoided. . . . You say I haven't spoken about this last manifestation of Bryan's. . . . I can't say all I think because even the English language has its limitations and I don't like to swear with pen and ink; it just seems unpleasant and gives no relief. My feelings on the matter you can readily guess, but there are two points that occur to me, full of importance: one, the power of the ignorant votes to spoil everything—the power to do that is the noblest privilege of democracy; and two, the effect all this discussion is going to have on religion. From his own point of view I can imagine nothing more stupid than Bryan's starting the question. The result will be exactly what he doesn't want. For him any discussion of Fundamentalism is likely to have unfortunate results, and in general those who think that nothing counts if the Bible loses its literal sanctity can only make trouble. The discussion had to come, but

think of Bryan's opening it. But he is stupid. . . .
It really depresses me that I can't write his life. The
one that ought to be written should go down the ages
like the plays of Aristophanes. William J. Bryan
would make a noble hero. But what good did the
plays of Aristophanes do? They were as ineffectual
as making faces at the enemy. Is there anything
sadder than Greek history? And the worst is, it
repeats itself at intervals. As for evolution, it interests me enormously. Our knowledge of it is as
vague and incomplete as is our knowledge of everything, but as we see it I find it fascinating, the most
inspiring thing I can imagine. It is such a relief to
see order everywhere. It makes no difference who
gave the order or when; one isn't made dizzy by
having everything whirling chaos. There is chaos
enough left. And the manifestations of evolution
are so thrillingly interesting to discover and to in-
vestigate. No, I have a tremendous respect for
science. Of course, there are many scientific men
who are fools—we are *all* miserable sinners—but that
doesn't hurt the glory of science in my eyes. Remember, it is the one manifestation of human thought in
which one struggles to find oneself wrong. That is
to its credit. I hate the world, but I don't know anything more fascinating. If it didn't exist I should
have to invent it—and then I should feel sorry. . . .

July 25. . . . It has been a great convenience
hitherto, to ascribe all our faults and shortcomings

To John T. Morse, Jr.

to the ignorant alien who threatened to swamp us all, but in fact the "alien" is, on the whole, pretty eager to get ahead, while the Yankee, who prided himself on being above superstition, takes the Bible for what Bryan and Co. says it is. He laughs at the degraded being who swallows what the priest says, and pins his faith to the Good Book as he reads it. The man who first mentioned liberty, equality and fraternity should have been broken on the wheel. Liberty of course we have not. No one would give five cents for fraternity. It is the day for equality, and to watch the garden-roller enforcing it is an interesting spectacle. In fact, the country is beginning to have the troubles by which a country is made something of value, something real, not a mere mass of insects, all shaped and thinking alike. Its stupid self-content and self-conceit must be shattered or at least shaken. . . .

July 31. . . . The whirl of gayety is not over, the Bishop and Lady deign to honour our humble home with their presence Wednesday evening next, at seven o'clock. M. brought home from her travels a wondrous set of waffle irons that work with astounding intelligence, the master-spirit being electricity, and we have promised to exhibit it on that occasion. The Bishop said he was afraid that waffles were fattening (he is just beginning to be that himself) but I, false friend, encouraged him by telling him that we haven't found them so. Mrs. Bishop said she

Thomas Sergeant Perry

wouldn't have a set in the house. . . . You say I said nothing about Bryan. You will live to regret the moment you opened that subject. How odd the notion of founding a college expressly not to teach evolution. Imagine the state of mind of the boys who won't wildly wonder what it is that is so perverting. It is impossible to imagine them deliberately shutting themselves off from the thought and knowledge of the time. The thing has only to be tried to fail. The plans should never be opposed. Give those fellows all they want; the walls they build will only tumble on them. It must have surprised W. J. B. not to have the sympathy of the R. C. church. He couldn't have expected the letters many of their priests have written on the subject. The position taken at Rome with regard to Modernism is exactly that of our own Fundamentalism. The only difference is that it really knocked down good men and made them apologise (Tyrrell, Ireland and others) and drove a lot of priests out of the church. He did exactly what Bryan would have liked to do. To have them objecting to him was amazing, but the old R. C. is wilier than W. J. B. and can sell in one market and buy in another. It has no narrow, exclusive system. Some men have to keep close to the catechism while others can believe nothing if that's what they like to do. All tastes are sacred, you can be a martyr or an atheist, so long as you keep quiet. All it really wants is a monopoly of transportation to the Great Beyond. Get into any of the cars you

To John T. Morse, Jr.

please; some of them are fitted with the newest books, but they are not to go outside of that car. Really, I think this whole Bryan business a most important event in the world's history. To have it break out in a country that has made men's head ache with the loud protestations of freedom and general education is one of those paradoxes that make this world really amusing. The notion of W. J. Torquemada Bryan popping up here and now—it's only the unexpected that happens, only the absurd. And from his own point of view what does he expect is going to happen when the credibility of Genesis is questioned? The whole dogma of Christianity rests on a very dubious tortoise. . . .

August 5. . . . It is a fearful responsibility having to take charge of a large part of this sinful world and then having to give you a few simple directions about the way the world is to be looked at, but it is my duty, and I will not shun it. In time I may lift even you out of the mire of ignorance and prejudice. My eloquence has already rescued you from your blind adoration of Bryan. You are, I feel sure, half disposed to break away from the Fundamentalists. For these steps upward I take to myself all the credit. It is really remarkable the way I have polished the rough diamond (you see, I am just) into a shape almost presentable. The thought of what I have done encourages me to go on. Thus, today I will call your attention to France, the ancient Gaul. That country seems to be anxious to be really progressive, and one of the notions is to give everyone an equal share in education and then an equal chance in life by modifying the higher schools, by leveling down in the good old way. There is to be no aristocracy anywhere. Bryan had in a coarser form the same abhorrence of anything savoring of aristocracy. He was well called the commoner. . . . The last elections the other day went mainly to the present radical government, in great measure by the abstention of the voters, and apparently there are going to be wild doings until the country takes a stand again. I would not choose this moment to lend money to the French. To discuss rather the mad social events in this eminent watering place, I will begin that we all lunch out today, at the cottage, where granddaughter Elsie will be our charming hostess. My! how the child talks. If all the Jacksons were kept in solitary confinement for one year and then all put in an iron pot and the cover removed, they wouldn't have half so much to say as she has all the time. Then to the evening meal come the Bishop and his lady—waffles! He is not allowed them at home for he is rounding out to fill the episcopal throne. . . .

August 18. . . . After all, it may well be that it is rash to despair because of the rowdiness of the young in these degenerate days. It prevails to a great extent as a twist of fashion, and in this country there is a mighty tendency to uniformity in thought and

To John T. Morse, Jr.

action, rather odd in a land that started out to establish liberty. It often occurs to me when I read the wails about the decay of the human race that perhaps we lose our tempers too speedily, and that nature is a great deal stronger than even fashion, and that the charming innocence of young girls will survive their follies. Do what they will, they won't turn themselves into men; they will remain very much what nature made them. One may be pretty sure of that. Waves of rowdiness have prevailed before, and like other waves, have died out, and when they were at their highest there was the great solid mass of the natural instinct of decency, which never got into print. Do I remind you of the abstracts of sermons which you see in the Monday morning papers? There is a certain resemblance, although they generally argue on the other side. If John Fiske (ahem!) were alive, I should go over to Cambridge and talk with him about something I was thinking about the other day, a proposition of reading human feelings into animal's actions. I was talking about it with the Bishop, I think it was, and it occurred to me, first, that there can exist no other feelings than those that agitate or inspire us, hope, desire, revenge, etc., and second, that the predominance of instinct prevents too much intellectual effort. One opposes the other, in human beings as in cats or whatever. Then, third, in animals that show the highest intelligence—rats, say, and elephants—well, here I become vague—possibly their brains are developed, in the case of rats, by meeting separate problems which the generalities of instinct would overcome less well than intelligence, etc., etc. I unduly compress my remarks, but J. F. would have discussed the matter most thoroughly and delightfully, for it was in his line. I am glad you are at Kennebunkport again, and I hope behaving properly. . . . I know your detestable nature and you won't be perfectly happy until you've killed yourself by overwork. But now when you have a chance to rest and store up strength, take it. It's the wisest plan. Do as I do! . . .

August 21. . . . I still think how you must have laughed at getting my white-washing letter about flappers and flapping, when your mind was so full of recent disclosures, as we might say. I still think these outbursts of the old Eve are sporadic, not endemic. They occur everywhere after the horror of war, as in the last century when the Napoleonic wars stopped; in Germany after the Thirty Years War; in England under Charles II. They go on until they arouse disgust and then there is a reaction to decency. This must come, for there is nothing more exhausting than a spree, and nothing surer to arouse long forgotten and utterly neglected moral sentiments; and then the general nature of young women is an innocent one, and taking it broad and large, nature is mightier than fashion, however indecent. You won't agree with me, but if I am wrong, then the world

To John T. Morse, Jr.

is following the march of the Hasty Pudding Club, altogether too fast. Of course, civilizations decay, and I often say this one is joining the Assyrian. Thus, venerable and dear Sir, if, by any chance you miss divine service Sunday, or in your attendance thereupon find the sermon a trifle dull, you have something to think about. Solve these questions and make the world happy, or perhaps unhappy. . . .

September 3. . . . You suggest a loftier subject when you ask who would live his life over again? Very few, I fancy, for it's a record of blunders, omitted good deeds, several misdeeds. No, we are all miserable sinners, and I suppose as bad as any would be the man who thought he had always lived as a model, if such a man ever existed. But, after all, man is not a ruminant, and he should never chew the cud, but he does and it only depresses him. As for the American voice, we seem to have taken it straight over from the war cry of the Indian. It is *dreadful,* and nothing so gets on my nerves. No one takes steps to correct it. Mothers answer their children's squalls with equal yells—it's awful. There is to me no charm like a beautiful speaking voice. I simply worshipped that of Adelaide Neilson. My grandchildren brought back, two out of three, a good voice from Europe, but America is doing its best to ruin them. This is a most melancholy P. S., but the subjects suggested by my spiritual adviser are not hilarious ones. I pause. . . .

Thomas Sergeant Perry

September 4. . . . To console me in these dark days I have received from Paris a new life of Horace Walpole, by a Frenchman, Paul Yvon, in 872 well-filled 8vo pages. The fashion seems to tend to long and stout books. This has the additional advantage of being readable. I read half a chapter last night and found it full of information and sufficiently intelligent. It was written by a lecturer at Caen for his doctorate, and those works are put together with no eye for the infirmities of the general reader, but solely to escape the microscopic eye of the professor who shall inspect the work. The writer leaves nothing unrecorded, and he has to put the vast heap into some presentable shape. One would think that H. W. could hardly fill a volume of this size. To fill it he would have to be beaten out like gold-beater's skin, and so it is. The book of course is as heavy as lead. It's like holding the ice-box to try to read it, so I can sip but a little at a time. While life is thus embittered, the sky is not wholly dark. I may be denied aesthetic joys, the doors of the concert hall may be closed to me, when I seek to forget my woes in study the mechanical difficulties may block me, but there is consolation, a rift in the clouds, the promise of better things; for last evening, I, unworthy as I am, forgotten of all save my gracious admirer [William Lyon] Phelps; I, whose identity is lost so utterly that I receive letters addressed to Thomas Cabot, Esq., I, who have drunk so deep a draught from the chalice of ignominy, have been asked to send to an unknown

To John T. Morse, Jr.

man—perhaps a fond, almost silent admirer—my *autograph*. He little knows how I treasure *his!*—how I leave his note open on my desk that not I alone may read it. I take it this distinction never came to you. It's simply impossible that it should, so you can't well understand my elation, but I am not selfish in my joy. I reflect on what a good thing it is for you. You will be able to turn my letters to some good use. You will be able to sell them for at least thirty-four cents apiece, and then you will laugh at the tax-gatherer. He, by the way, expects to collect the trifle of two billions from people who haven't paid enough. Your uneasiness is natural. I was once pursued in that way. I gave the demon a good cigar and half an hour's delightful conversation and have never heard from him since. Be then of good cheer. . . .

September 7. . . . Another anecdote told by Jim McLane was of seeing ——, who has bought a farm. You go as near it as you can in your car, then get out and walk a mile. ——kept a cow, but after a short time found the cow gone dry. He sought the aid of experts. They asked him how often he milked the cow. "Oh, not very often, only when someone wanted some milk.". . . I suppose you who have been to fashionable watering-places will not be so surprised as I was on getting away from savagery to the sight of the way women now dress themselves in town. The opening of my eyes began in Lowell (and I never made so short a stay in that interesting town. The chauffeur knew how to get away) and there I saw ladies arrayed in bath towels, table-cloths and apparently their brother's undershirts, walking as calmly, with much display of unbeautiful legs, as if they were really dressed. Of course, it was the same thing in town. I am afraid I am dreadfully old-fashioned, but while I fully recognize the fitness of the pillow-case for its avowed purpose, I fail to see its charm as an article of dress. Of course, every woman will tell me it's the most beautiful thing in the world. I wonder it was discovered so late. The whole effect recalled to me an opera ball to which those wild rakes, J. Mills Pierce and William Ware, lured me in the sad days of the Second Empire—there nine-tenths of the ladies were one-tenth clad in the elegant simplicity of the chemise. We seem to be returning to that style of dress, which, even then, in Paris, under the Empire, was thought eccentric. . . .

September 9. . . . And now the barrel is empty, the lamp burns low, the gas is gone and there is no red pump near where one may fill the tank. I am stalled and no further progress is to be made. It's curious what a rumpus that Tennessee case has made. It has brought face to face the two contestants and has forced a good many people to think, which is exactly what Bryan didn't want them to do. The Nebraska Professor says there are ten millions who

To John T. Morse, Jr.

agree with him, and I dare say he is right. In England the question has risen more or less, and it's curious to see how much further advanced is the intelligent comprehension there than here. Of course, the aged always mourn, but it seems true that this country is in a state of intellectual feebleness. Charles Norton, the Jeremiah of his time, was no further from true patriotism than I am. If justice existed in this country, I should be burned at the stake on Boston Common. It would be a good end for me and great fun for the newspapers. How minutely the reporters would describe the process of combustion, and the photographers would perpetually apply their interesting art. Doubtless you would stay away from the vulgar ceremony, but sometime you would go to see it represented in the movies. In the dark room no one would notice that you were there, and if they did, few would think it strange. They would remember that you knew me well and would think it only natural that you should go at least once. . . .

September 26. . . . As a lover of animals, as that noble thing, a farmer (though in the past), as a son of New England, it may interest you to hear of a new step to bring this part of the country into something like its old importance. Read and you will understand. Yesterday I went out from the house and lifting my eyes I saw before me a full-grown sheep. I shuddered and stood still, for although it was tethered, I feared it might attack me and bite my leg. I asked, quoting William Blake's poem: "Little Lamb, who made thee?" but I got no answer, and its appearance baffled me till M. told me it was a present from a kind neighbour. It will be handy when anyone runs in and the larder is empty. We can find a chop always at hand without running to Peterborough. What may be left of it is to spend the winter in the barn, which will be more like the ark than ever with six cows, one horse, a heifer and a cat; for Scampo is again to spend the winter here rather than languishing in town. I have told M. about the offer of the Government to give a pair of buffalo to any good citizen who loves animals and will take care of them. . . .

October 7, 1925. The world being what it is, it is only natural that in times of defeat and depression many should in despair crowd into monasteries as the only abodes of peace and comfort. Behind that wall they were safe and there many of them believed, or tried to believe, that they were thus saving their souls. At any rate they applied for this boon just as men who have retired from work claim a dole. These emotions are called forth by your letter and its facts. Why shouldn't I go to a monastery? I have received no circulars about them—they are the only industry that hasn't sent me circulars—but I know that some exist. I may yet knock at the door, which I have often entered, at the monastery of St.

To John T. Morse, Jr.

John the Evangelist in Staniford St. There are, to be sure, many disadvantages: the absence of bath tubs, the meagre fare, the early hours—still, I am not in this last respect sunk in so deep a mire as some we might mention.—What I want is to go to a monastery in the country. I don't wonder men flocked to them. They must have seemed like a dignified poorhouse, or Old Man's Home, and in such a place—given a good table—I could bid farewell to the world's vanities. . . .

October 19, '25. . . . The birds are amusing. I don't know how late woodpeckers stay, whether they pass the winter here or in Virginia, but I saw one the other day. The chickadees are beginning to flutter about, after a summer at the N. Pole. They are an amusing bird. It breaks my heart to think that there is all this life about us and that we can't touch it, can get into no real relation with it, except perhaps as not bullying it or feeding it. Still I might be disappointed; I might find them just like human beings. . . .

September 3, 1927. . . . I agree with you in detestation of fliers, who combine with the baseball players to make so much of the papers unreadable. It is to be remembered, however, that at the present rate of mortality among them there will very soon be no one left to fly and the world will relapse into its old ways of travelling, which are, some of them, dangerous enough. I wonder if you received from the Philosophic Department of the Stanford University a lot of questions which were meant to bring out answers that should prove a warning to future generations. Probably not, for it was sent only to the truly eminent, like me, and no construction of the conditions set would let you in. Hence I will tell you about it and you will see what a price we pay for being famous and you will be contented in your obscurity. I am asked, for instance, whether one of my activities is pursuing bandits in a sheriff's posse or acting as yell-leader, and I am asked to express my feeling—like, dislike or indifference to—this sport and a lot of others. I won't go on, but really if that is education, give me the company of savages. I shan't answer the thing, of course, any more than you will yours, for I'm afraid that my answers might be objectionable. Really, for once I feel almost impatient, though I confess it is amusing to be spoken of as a successful business man! It is the first time I have encountered such ingenious flattery. . . .

October 4. . . . You speak of Miss Bell's letters. I have not seen them. They are barely out, but I know they will be well worth reading. It's odd, Americans are said to sacrifice themselves for their womankind, to let them have all the education or culture going, to put them on a pedestal, to let them do whatever they please, while the Englishwoman is a sort of slave, but, by Jingo! we don't produce any-

To John T. Morse, Jr.

thing like some of the great English women. This Miss Bell, of whom Camperdown told you, was a most extraordinary woman, of vast influence in the East. I'm sure you will be immensely interested in her letters and find there something you never saw before. Our Mrs. Catt is a less glorious being. I saw in yesterday's *Times* that a woman in charge of a census in a New York County, gave all the fat jobs to her relatives and cost the county about three times the right price. She seems to have for a moment forgotten that women were ordered by Heaven to purify politics. I have been reading with great delight Godley's *Reliquiae,* 2 vols., a medley of articles on Greek and Latin in the universities, of travel in Greece, of climbing the Alps, of amusing poems and some beautiful Latin—he was University orator in Oxford—a curious hodge-podge, but entertaining. Miss Bell's letters are something real and I know will interest you. . . . Your selections from the *Wall Street Journal* are, as always, capital reading. It's odd how the paper is never mentioned by its esteemed contemporaries, any more than were Luther's pamphlets by ecclesiastics in Rome. Thus, one sees how in a country that boasts its freedom, one fears to arouse the wholly imaginary indignation of the masses by mention of this journal. It's interesting to see how this indignation rests on the notion that the money of Wall Street belongs exclusively to Morgan & Co.— a good deal of it does, but not all. In short, this world is full of sickening humbug. Thus, I receive today a postcard from Prof. ——, of Stanford University, regretting that I did not fill out his blank about the interests of my boyhood—a lot of utterly foolish questions, which I threw into the waste paper basket. Now he offers to send me another blank. Why does he bother me? I don't want to be rude or to hurt his feelings, but I must answer him and I shall do so, trying hard to be civil. Of course I shan't answer the questions, and I doubt the right of entire strangers to buttonhole me and ask irrelevant queries. He reminds me of the young man at the Harvard Club, who walked up to me and, without any introduction, asked me how old I was. He won't ask that question again so suddenly of anyone. The political talk is as dull as this letter. Why the country should rise and turn out the Republicans, bad as they are, to put in a lot of Democratic officials, hungry and ignorant, I can't see. There is one comfort in submitting to a dictator, one doesn't have this absurd election rumpus every five minutes. . . .

October 6. . . . I read once more Macaulay's Addison and Mme. d'Arblay last evening, and with the same enthusiasm as I felt the first time, because M. always gets you there, so to speak. He knows what he wants to say and he says it, you hear him and understand him. He has no shavings left from his work. He is never dull for a moment and often is delightfully vivacious. It is not the only way of writing, but it is a great way. He may have every

To John T. Morse, Jr.

fault they charge him with: prejudice, inaccuracy, etc., etc., for he is human, but few beings are as seldom dull as he is. He was a wonderful creature. The Addison interested me particularly at this moment, for I have just been reading a most villainous attack on him by a new, and I judge, young Englishman named Dobrée. He is attacked as the first Victorian, and hence contemptible. Poor A., who after the time of Rochester, Sedley, etc., tried to show people the ways of decency, is now to be despised for it. It was a curious assault, the real animus was the twentieth century's hate of the nineteenth. You and I have lived to see two such incidents. We sneered at the poor old Eighteenth, and seemed to have got the world on its right end at last—not a bit of it, all the boys nowadays are eager to show you what a series of mistakes we made, what humbugs we all were. This contempt every generation has for the one before—so one laughs at one's parents—does however keep things moving. The Chinese are bound to worship their ancestors—is that the reason of the stagnation there? Such and many other thoughts rise within me. We shall never see the twentieth century criticised, but I think I know what the twenty-first will say. . . .

Nov. 17. . . . I don't know whether you have finished Ludwig's *Bismarck,* but in any case I am sure you have found lots of interesting things in the book. I am more than half way through it and I read it with something like rapture. German politics of sixty years ago have only "local" interest and at that time were very puzzling. When W. James and I were in Berlin, we used to read the *National Zeitung* every morning, partly to improve our German, partly to understand things, but I confess I could never quite make out what it was all about. I knew that old Bismarck was widely hated and widely admired. All the inner complications were hidden. This book answers many of the questions of that day. What a man he was! And what a country he lived in! What a picture is given us of a politically crude land! One can see all Teutonic qualities that brought them to 1918. It is a lamentable thing when a country finds the growth of its strength exceeds that of its intelligence, as was the case with them then, and is now with us. Life on this globe is beset by so many perils that a careful intelligence is needed to keep things straight, and where do we find it? In the Senate? Under whose hat? In political leaders anywhere? And yet arrogance and unreasonableness are growing all the time. To go back to Bismarck, what a curious mixture he was. I confess all human beings are that, though not always in such picturesque colours. And what a head! . . . You haven't seen Mark Sullivan's books, in which he tries to portray those ancient days, i.e., 1900. He collects various things from the newspapers and pinning them together says he has made a complete picture of the times. He has done nothing of the sort, he has simply made a more or less inter-

To John T. Morse, Jr.

esting scrap-book. I wonder if any history ever gets any nearer to the truth. You know what I think history should be, and, for that matter, often is, a means of entertainment like the Arabian Nights, and to some extent of instruction, like the parables. Exact truth is the last thing one should demand of it. It should tell true things, but not undertake to explain them. I used to make Rhodes' life miserable by pointing out how hard it was to get the exact facts without any care for their meaning. You know I like histories that tell me what I want to hear, the destruction of the Armada, the defeat of the Germans in 1918. Bill Thompson shares my views perfectly. He wants histories full of patriotism. He is a great man, and I am—Yours always. . . . P. S. It's curious to see the incoherence of Senator Glass's discrimination between the Fifteenth and Eighteenth Amendments. No one for a moment imagines that they are alike— why should they be? An amendment is supposed to make clean work. The point that they make is that the Eighteenth, being made, should be observed as law by all. In that case, the Fifteenth, having been passed, is also law and demands compliance. The thing too plain, one would think, to be mistaken.

VII

(To Salomon Reinach)

Boston, December 12, 1914. Dear Mr. Reinach: I can't tell you how often I have thought of you since I left Paris, and especially since this war began; and I must write a line to tell you how thoroughly all our sympathies go with you in this struggle. I have never seen such unanimity in the community. In our own Civil War there was very much more diversity of opinion, even here in Boston, which was perhaps the centre of opposition to the South. The one or two pro-Germans find no approval. Nor does the feeling rest there. . . . The fact is that we feel that you are fighting our war. Your men at the front are defending us, you are protecting everything that makes life precious for us. You are guarding civilization. It is terrible to think not merely of the mourning and suffering, but, after these are stilled, the direct loss to civilization of so many eager young lives with so many plans and so much competence to perform them. The blighting effects of war last very long. . . .

Hancock, N. H., Sept. 14, 1916. Just as a foreigner during the war has to report himself from time to

To Salomon Reinach

time to the authorities, so I feel that I ought occasionally write to my friends that I am still thinking of them and of the cause for which they are fighting, with no change of heart. . . . The worst cases here are some of the professors who went to Germany as part of the exchange. The Kaiser was thoughtful enough to show them civility and their heads were turned. I have always said that while all like flattery, none drink the poisoned draught with half the zest of Americans, for we never use it ourselves in our treatment of one another. We employ instead the very opposite thing; we chaff one another and pretend to despise our friends. The consequence is that when an American is treated civilly, by an Emperor especially, these unaccustomed words are honey to his ears. He says, "What a judge of character that man is!" and he purrs audibly. Poor man! Any foreigner would simply smile and begin to ask himself, "What is it the man wants of me that he is so civil?" ——, whose book I sent you, is pro-German. I see him and we belong to the same dining club, but we never mention the war to him. Sometimes at the Club dinners he has to endure opposing views. Then there is the ridiculous ——, a professor, once of Columbia, I believe. . . . As for the Irish and their frantic denunciations of England, it's but the screaming of naughty children and has no influence. . . . The fact is not many Americans know at all what Europe is. . . . I have been reading Doudan's letters, do you know them? They came out about forty years ago and made a great impression on me. I have been reading them over this summer, and it is curious to observe how clearly he saw the Germans and their nature long ago. He had no delusions about them. But why be so clear-sighted? Cassandra's fate is well known. This country swarms with amiable people who think war will be prevented by holding up your hands. . . . I should not be allowed to fight, but I have a nephew in the ambulance service "somewhere in France." I told him it was the best thing he could do.

Boston, November 28, 1916. . . . There are those who think they serve civilization by abandoning all effort to preserve it, and these are the vast masses in the West who wholly misunderstood the war and care very little about it. They are the men who elected Wilson the other day. In the whole country they are a minority who understand the German peril, who know that you are fighting our battle for us. There are many reasons for this. Few people think at all, and then they see so much prosperity coming to them from the war that they overlook its horrors. Only a day or two ago a man was overheard to say in a train, "I couldn't believe that I should ever make so much money as I have done this year. Every night I pray that the war may go on for a hundred years."—As for voting for Wilson there is this illustrative anecdote. A friend of mine said to a man in

To Salomon Reinach

a New Hampshire village, "There goes so and so, I am sure he will vote the Republican ticket."—The answer was, "I am not so sure. You see in old times when a critter (cow) died, he would sell the hide for two dollars. This year he got ten dollars for one, and he thinks Wilson has done it." And yet there are people who think every question should be settled by those people.—Tonight there is to be a great meeting to protest against the deportation of the Belgians. The Germans will never understand our feelings. They are so constituted that they think that whatever they want to do is right, because they want to do it. That wish is enough. . . . . .

Boston, May 14, 1917. I am enclosing an article from a Boston paper that will show you how a great many people feel about the authorities in Washington and especially about the President. For my part I have very little confidence in him. I feel that he regards this war as sent by heaven to give him a chance to acquire lasting fame, and that he will do everything with that aim steadfastly in view. I have not forgiven him for urging peace without victory and for his silence earlier in the war, his definition of neutrality, his ignorance of the causes of the war, etc. At any rate, here we are in the war, and much of the shame I had been feeling is now gone. So far we are only in the talking condition. I hope soon we shall be of real practical use. It was time to come in when poor old absurd Russia fell flat. Let us be thankful that Leo Tolstoy is not alive to preach brotherly love. . . .

Hancock, July 31. . . . What will be the fate of Russia, in this war at least, is a puzzling question. If anything is needed to fasten a Kaiser in his throne, the present conduct of Russia will supply it. After all, what is it but establishing the democracy we all say that we are fighting for? . . . The condition of affairs in Philadelphia, as in most American cities, is an excellent example of the charm of democracy to be added to the confusion in Russia. Not that Russia surprises me, what else could be expected from so ignorant a people after so long a despotism?—All these things happen and yet people laugh at the old English tragedians for inventing impossibilities. It is life that finds them and prevents them. The wildest imaginations are impotent by the side of facts. The wildest romanticist is the only true realist. This brings us to rank Hegelianism. . . .

Boston, February 6, 1918. . . . It seems to me as if civilization were doomed, our civilization at least, and that we who had known the days before this war had known something which would not be equalled for many long years. It may be a good thing for this civilization to go, but I am sorry to part with it, such as it was. Don't imagine me too much depressed; I have always been a confirmed pessimist

To Salomon Reinach

and am now full of satisfaction with finding all my forebodings justified, and with regard to the outcome of this war I am always an optimist. Meanwhile, I search for a book worth reading. They are rare. I hope the time may come when I shall get back to Paris. . . .

Hancock, June 26. There are so many things I could talk about to you that I am embarrassed at beginning a letter to know what to choose. The one thing however that has been before me all this while since I last wrote has been our delay in getting men over to you. I have suffered agonies of shame and regret that so much time was wasted in repressing preparation and denouncing those who urged it, a process not yet finished. Of late, great efforts have been made and there are a good many Americans in France, I hope not too late. I hear, indeed, that W. W. is at last determined to carry the war through. For a long time there was hesitation, and even now in Washington there are in high quarters men who are forever holding back and standing for the first chance to preach the charms of peace. . . . I hope the American troops do not make themselves obnoxious by bragging. There are those who don't brag, and then those who do. The papers are full of it, under the impression that it keeps up the spirits of their readers. It saddens mine. But I won't talk about the war. Let me rather ask you if you have ever seen the *Memoirs of William Hickey,* 2 vols.,

Blackett. Hickey was an unknown man and in his youth at least, very naughty, but he has written, very unconsciously, a capital story of his life. It reads almost as well as Robinson Crusoe. I am sure you would like it. He was born in 1749. I have read only Vol. I, so I can't say exactly when it was written, but apparently about one hundred years ago, at the age of sixty. . . .

August 15. Your most welcome letter brought me great consolation, for it showed that after all some American soldiers had got over in time. They are a nice looking lot in the unified appearance that a uniform always gives, and life in this country gives every one of them the habit of meeting novel conditions and of adapting himself to them. I wish there were more of them with you. If the government could have acted sooner, if W. W. had not spent so much time in trying to be an angel of peace! One hears it said that the people would not have followed him if he had counselled war. I cannot think so. The voice of authority is very persuasive, and when I consider how effective was his unnatural advice to us "to be neutral in our hearts," I am sure that a call to war would have aroused everyone. People love to be told what to do (hence the Church of Rome among other things). For an example, at the beginning of the war, when my wife asked the women in this village to join with her in making bandages, clothes, etc., for the Belgians—we to supply the

To Salomon Reinach

material—some excellent women feared lest they should cease to be perfectly neutral in their hearts. But they yielded to argument, and have ever since worked busily. Roosevelt, or even Taft, would have brought us into the war sooner and with better result. I can't bear to think how future historians will always call this the *late* war.—Do you know Lord Charnwood's *Lincoln?* It is a delightful book, full of information imparted with wisdom and intelligence. It's curious how few books are written by intelligent people, and what a charm their intelligence gives to their work. Sometimes it seems as if only the stupid people wrote books in a vain effort to get away from their own dullness. This book gives an admirable picture of Lincoln and of his whole period; it will help the reader to understand this country. As to the Hickey memoirs, there is no doubt in my mind of their genuineness; the man who could invent them would make his fortune as a novelist. These two volumes read like Robinson Crusoe in the chronicling of incidents and the absence of anything but the simplest psychology. The most suspicious thing is his extraordinary memory of names. Writing after a long and busy interval, he recalls fellow-revellers, as if he had dined with them last week. Less surprising is his recollection of the various dishes and wines at remote banquets. There could be no reason for inventing these memoirs. He touches historical persons and events only very lightly. One of the most interesting of these references is to Mrs. Grand, afterwards Mme. de Talleyrand. The light it throws on English society is interesting, especially their hideous habit of practical joking—and how they did drink! If this war ever ends, and I don't, I hope to get to Paris and to have a long talk with you.

Hancock, October 5. Let me thank you for your *Chronologie de la Guerre* (Vol. VII) just received. It is a capital condensation of the whole story. Indeed, I have often thought that properly conducted annals would be a thousand times better than the literary histories which are generally written to teach some lesson, to defend some hobby of the historian; thus Grote, Lingard, in fact almost all of them. When I am admitted to the company of writers of history, I endear myself to them by proving the hollowness of all of their methods. Even those who rest on the boasted documents are no better than the others, for what newspaper, for example, gets the exact truth? I was amused the other day to see in a French journal (*L'Opinion*) a letter from a man who had been trying to find just what Malvy said at the end of his trial. He looked at fifty papers and no two agree....

October 17. I wrote to my friend Senator Lodge the other day, asking him to send you his later speeches in the Senate, and I think they will interest you. He is very sound on all the questions now agitating us. We had a great fright the other day when W. W. thought it well to answer the first Ger-

To Salomon Reinach

man note with questions, as if he was beginning a long debate. The whole country was aroused, and it became so clear that this was not what was wanted, that the President became more rigid and answered with some firmness. You know what Root said of him, that he first shakes his fist in their face and then a finger. . . . I lost another nephew the other day in action, Franklin Pepper, my sister's son. My brother's son, Franklin Perry, died some months ago. They had a right to the name of Franklin, being great-great-great grandsons of Benjamin Franklin. He would have been contented with their fighting in France. . . .

Boston, December 14. At last I am in my own house, after a long series of visits, and I can sit down comfortably and answer your most welcome letter. You meanwhile are doubtless making yourself hoarse with cheers for Mr. Wilson. The feeling about him here is very different from that which appears in Europe. The Germans seem to regard him as an American uncle who will do whatever they want, and he seems to be highly thought of everywhere, though what those who are to meet him at the council-table really think of him they of course don't say. In this country there is no such enthusiasm. He has a few adorers who say it is our duty to support him, whatever he does, but he has succeeded in arousing a general, an almost universal distrust. All the intelligentsia lack confidence in him. The general opinion is that the one thing he cares for is himself, that he will visit the Pope to win the Catholic vote, will humour the Irish for their votes and be humane to the Germans for theirs. He is thought to be very clever, but a man without principle. His attitude for so long a time to the war showed his character; he was driven by the popular feeling to act as he finally did. He is himself without feeling, and takes very seriously the flattery he has received from Europe. He surrounds himself with inferior men. . . . Fortunately for France and for the world he will encounter sturdier men who really care for their task and not for what profit it may bring them. They will take his measure. They will be gentle with him, because perhaps they may think he represents the country, but they need not be too careful of him. He is not trusted here. I am not expressing the mere growl of the opposition, I am telling you the general thought of the country. I could give you many instances of his pettiness, of his vindictiveness, but you have doubtless heard too much already.

What a blessing that the war is over! I have no sudden joy about it, the change has been like the advent of a new season. I gradually learn not to expect new horrors every day. There may be plenty, and I am very sure that we who saw the time between the two German-French wars saw what was for a great part of the world the Golden Age. All thought, all intellectual life has known so severe a shock that I wonder when they will move smoothly again. There

To Salomon Reinach

will be so many trying to make the world better that everything will be spoiled. I saw the other day a paragraph written by a man who rejoiced that in changes wrought in the world was reformed spelling, and he was happy.—You will notice that here already has begun a cry for a larger navy, as large as the British. That does not promise ease for a tortured world, but there is no popular enthusiasm behind it. For one thing taxes are not popular. Thanks for your good *Chronologie,* it is capital reading, and I look forward to the next volume as the best reading of the lot. What a superb story it will make of one blow after another till the crash came. The real solution of the trouble would be that which Rome applied to Carthage. Any other treatment simply invited a renewal of the game.—I have been reading Glover on Virgil and am now delighted with Goumy's book, *Les Latins,* which I have just got hold of. I don't know when we shall get abroad again, but a visit to France is among the possibilities.—Farewell. Love Wilson and be happy. I detest his English style, it is so odiously clerical. . . .

January 30, 1919. . . . I am only now beginning to comprehend that the war is, apparently, over. At first the statement of its ending was something like telling me that the sun was so many million miles from the earth, which, however true, means nothing to me, but now my dull mind is opening to it, and I breathe more easily. . . .

Thomas Sergeant Perry

February 24. . . . Here there is much talk of Class War, and Bolsheviki, etc., etc., and there are those who advocate doing everything you know to be unwise in order to avert these various perils. Perhaps they are right, but if there is to be a war, it is not well to enter it frightened to death. You know what bluff is; one can see a great deal of it lying about everywhere now.—I have been reading over various papers in your *Cultes, Mythes,* etc., with the greatest pleasure. Shall we ever get back to the civilization of before the war? I sometimes, often indeed, doubt it. Certainly this country does not promise much, nor does it perform much.—I will not longer croak. Have you seen Irvin Cobbs' *Glory of the Coming?* It is a capital book; humorous, but yet without running on too long; pathetic, but not too harrowing, and describing things very well indeed. It contains charming things about both England and France. If you don't know the book, please let me know and I will send it to you. I think it quite remarkable. . . .

March 9. I received your most interesting letter of February 11th a few days ago, and last evening came the *Chronologie,* Vol. VIII, and I at once read it as one reads the agonizing fourth act of a play that one knows ends well. It was indeed an anxious time, and for my part I was always suppressing my joy lest I should be disappointed by a successful stand of the Germans at some strong line. I think too that a brief

To Salomon Reinach

chronicle like yours is perhaps the best way of writing history. You have the facts and you can make any use of them you will; whereas history, as it is usually written, goes to strengthen some preconception of the historian—examples are many. The Roman annals, then, and your *Chronologie* show what history would have been but for the baneful effect of Hellenic literary enthusiasm.—You ask why there arose in this country that wave of ill-feeling towards France, but I can give no answer. It seems to have passed off as mysteriously as it appeared. Of course all relations of human beings to one another are liable to go wrong, from Cain and Abel down. Two nations find it very hard to understand each other, and are annoyed by the pettiest trifles. I am sure there must be great annoyance in France with the absolute absence of any pretense of good manners among the Americans, just as the Americans must have thought the polite ways of the French were mere vehicles of deceit. . . . France is not well known here. Few travellers see more than the shops, the theatres and the dance-halls. It is surprising how many there are who can't read French easily and what multitudes who are ignorant of French life and taste, of the incessant toil and acute judgment of the French people. They don't understand the beautiful French civilisation, but they will understand it better after the war. I have seen in country newspapers letters from soldiers that showed a new understanding of France. Still I must remember that there is a good deal of ignorance about a great many things. It is the normal state of man. . . . The President has made a week-end visit here and is off again. He has no tact. By a little rudimentary courtesy he might have the Senate meeting him half way, but he lost his temper and began to threaten most unwisely. He has the nature of a despot, and he forgot to discuss the projected league. He tried to force it, on his recommendation, on the Senate. It was most unwise. The Senate would probably agree that some league must be formed, but they object very naturally to accepting this rough draft as a final word. It will be discussed by Lodge and Lowell (president of Harvard College) and I will send you the report of their remarks. The schism is most unfortunate, and might have been, if not avoided, at least mollified by a less imperious tone on the part of the President. . . .

March 17. Thanks for the paper on *Eve* which reached me day or two ago, having come by a slower ship. These odd delays frequently occur with my French papers. You need have no fear of your treatment of the delicate subject. The paper could be read aloud in a girl's boarding-school without provoking a blush. It's a curious point you bring out, in fact you never fail to do that any more than you fail to show your wide reading. I am sending you the speech of Lodge about the League. In fact I send a pamphlet containing many speeches, all the documents, on the case. There are, of course, many who

To Salomon Reinach

accept W. W.'s words as heaven sent, but there are others who are enraged by his determination to force his will through without explanation or further consideration. Some of Lodge's objections seem to me very sound, but W. W. hates Lodge. Lodge was asked to make an address at some celebration at Johns Hopkins University and the President was invited. He sent word that he couldn't come if Lodge was to be prominent—giving them a chance to suggest to Lodge to stay away—but they did nothing. Lodge spoke and the President was not there. There is to be a great debate Wednesday evening between Lodge and Lawrence Lowell on the League. . . . I shall not hear them, for the call for tickets is tremendous, and moreover I am more accustomed to reading than to listening to long orations. I dine with Lodge Friday evening and shall have a chance to talk things over with him, for we shall be but six at table.— W. W. sems to me to show very poor taste in not giving more credit to the French and British troops for their long struggle, but what can you expect of a man who not so long ago said he could see no great difference between the aims of the allies and those of their opponents? If that man ever feels remorse, he must find it hard to choose any of his utterances before the war to think of with approval. But you know my state of mind about that man, and I forbear to go on.—What with the newspapers and my incessant yawps on the faults of my betters, your life will be miserable. It's no wonder that you run to the Fathers, even to the theological subtleties, to distract your mind from the questions of today. . . .

Hancock, July 19. . . . I am glad whenever G. B. Shaw gets the treatment he deserves. He is a curiously unsatisfactory person, as clever as he can be, and perfectly hateful. His attitude in the war is that of Ireland immensely magnified. . . . The politicians want the Irish vote, and so affect sympathy; the newspapers hate to say what they think, lest their subscriptions fall off, and in general the American is a timid soul; so that we all seem most enthusiastic for the Irish republic, whereas we know it would mean only another form of quarreling. Yet no one dares to bring out the Irish sympathy (and more) for the Germans in the war.—We have peace, but what the Senate here will do, is very uncertain. I think the treaty will be ratified with some unimportant changes. W. W. has managed the whole business with very little wisdom; he has made enemies right and left, so that the merits of his case have sunk into the background. He tried to impose his scheme on the world because it was his, and his obstinacy infuriates his opponents and annoys his supporters. He is devoid of tact to a degree that is agonizing. Those who are opposing him are gradually being forced into line with the wildest socialists who think him too severe to Germany! The whole discussion is very painful, it brings out abuse of England (as controlling this government), of France (as

To Salomon Reinach

Imperialistic), and generally destroys what good might have come from the war. The hatred between different nations was inevitable, and human nature makes everyone hate what he can't understand. . . . After all, it is a vile world we live in. The only comfortable thing is to try to forget it, but when everyone neglects it, it only becomes even worse. . . .

July 23. I received the final volume of your *Chronologie* yesterday, and I have read a great deal of it—thank heaven, not all—with immense delight. You had here a charming subject which one will never be tired of reading, for your story comes out right, and there is a good deal to be said in favour of a happy ending. I prefer to take my history that way. I like to read the account of the Spanish Armada better than that of the Sicilian expedition. There is a good deal, too, to be said in favour of your way of writing history, in the form of annals. You give the material and let the reader make up his own mind. That is the way the Romans began, but later they were poisoned by Greek arts, and one can hardly believe a word they say.—Historians speak of history as a science; it is really something like philosophy, the writer's impression of the past with the preaching the historian is inspired to utter. What the historian really teaches us is the state of his mind. I am violent in this matter, and I never see an historian without attacking him in some such way as this. I vainly hope to do him good.—The opposition to the League seems too great for opposition. I am sorry, because it begets coldness to England and France and can only aid Germany, but the whole question has become one of parties, and nothing else is thought of. If Wilson had been a different man there might have been no trouble, but tact cannot be learned. There were, of course, many good objections to the League, but nothing is perfect and it is depressing to see the winning of the war frittered away in defeat.—I noticed what you said about poisons in future wars. The Germans will look after that. . . .

August 21. . . . I should say in general that the American, though totally without manners, is a kind creature. I see that continually. I wonder what you thought of Irvin Cobb's book. It has a quality that smacks of the soil, and I wish I knew how it struck you.—Of late I have been trying to forget the world we live in, with its strikes and quarrels, and have found solace in that most delightful book, Chuquet's *Stendhal-Beyle.* I had read B. of course, and a good deal that had been written about him, and hesitated to take up this ponderous tome—there is so much *snobisme* in the way his washing-lists have been exhumed and printed—but having done so, I am more content. I didn't know that there was so good a book left for me to read. The only fault I find with it is that it is too short. If Chuquet had written a life of Voltaire on this pattern, what a book it would have been! As it is, he has produced a large 8vo volume

To Salomon Reinach

of 550 pages, and not a dull word in it. I have read Arthur Tilley's *Dawn of the French Renaissance,* very worthy doubtless, but wholly without charm.— One has to find comfort in books, for the contemplation of events is not soothing. It sems to me evident that Germany is at its usual trick of trying to ruin the world by propaganda. In this country the foolish good nature of the people and the timidity of politicians are having the worst effect at present. . . .

August 22. It is an abominable habit I have of giving you no peace, of pursuing you with letters, but I must speak to you about the *Athenæum,* which, of course, you see. I gave it up during the war when it gave all its attention to sociology, but I subscribed again when it started on its new task. Don't you find it very interesting? These new men seem to be trying to save what they can of our tottering civilisation and their earnestness interests me greatly. They seem to have very definite ideas and to put them well on the page. They have a noble task, all the harder because they have lost so many who would have stood by them. It is interesting to see a new movement. To be sure the misguided youths are unanimous in sneering at the Victorian epoch, not knowing what they miss in not sharing our cigars, India paper, books and moderate prices.—Their writing seems to me to have a quality which heretofore I have seen only in the best French work, a product of ripe civilization. They know foreign things but are not overwhelmed by them. It is a pleasant day when I get my *Athenæum* and the Literary Supplement of the *Times*. It's like sitting and hearing good talk, which is the greatest pleasure the world knows. One finds nothing of the sort in this unhappy country, and less, as time goes on, rather than more. . . .

November 26. The conduct of the Senate with regard to the treaty must be very puzzling to the French, as it is to us, indeed. . . . The Senate is a body very jealous of its rights, and will not receive orders from the President. I asked Cabot Lodge if everything would not have gone smoothly if W. W. had now shown any tact, and he said, "Certainly it would."—Lodge, who is a fighter, put venom into the matter, and introduced political prejudice as politicians are sure to do, and the result is the present unhappy state of affairs. Now if the President makes any sign of yielding his extravagant pretensions, there will be a speedy and satisfactory solution, but he is a very obstinate man. You will understand, I am defending neither side, I merely state what I think the cause of the unhappy dissension. . . .

Boston, January 29, 1920. . . . I am reading Taine's *Correspondance* with great interest. It is not necessary to agree with him to see what a fine creature he was, and how well he shows those delightful qualities of the French which they hide from a hasty glance by pretending in their novels and plays to be

To Salomon Reinach

merely frivolous. I should have read the book some years ago, but I was in Paris and I couldn't get hold of it. Here the Public Library gets whatever I want and is glad to have the book. . . . Meanwhile time is passing and has taken with it a good part of my sense of hearing. My consolation is how many foolish remarks I miss, and how few wise ones. In Paris I should miss more wise ones, and in conversation it is, of course, important to know what the other fellow is saying. I am not complaining; in the course of my life I have heard much good talk, and none better than *chez vous* in Paris.—You know the condition of things here, W. W. still mysteriously ill, and a new President to be chosen, with the whole world in confusion. I suppose in time it will settle down.

March 25. Feeling as I do about the disgraceful conduct of America toward the treaty, I find myself almost ashamed to write to anyone in Europe. The world is falling and our political leaders are fighting like cocks in the barnyard. I won't bore you with the long screed that is boiling within me, but will at once quote for you a detached note I found in a reprint, or perhaps the first printing, of the Journals of Washington Irving, July '15—July '42, published by the Boston Bibliophile Society. The Journals are mere scrappy memoranda, of no possible interest, except this one sentence put down in 1823. "Remark of an Advocate at Aix-la-Chapelle: 'The Prussians have done in two years what Bonaparte for the French could not in twenty-five. They have caused the French to be loved.'" Vol. I, p. 222. I thought that might amuse you.—Since I can't be in France, I do the best I can by reading French books. At this moment I am greatly enjoying G. Lanson's *Life of Voltaire*. There is a good life of Voltaire written by an American, James Parton, about fifty years ago. . . .

May 26. . . . This country is plunging deeper and deeper into the mire and giving the world a very good view of the value of a much-vaunted democracy. It is a shameful condition of things, and it will be worse next autumn. . . . You are right in saying no foreigner appreciates Racine. I have never known one who did. I don't, yet I perceive the charm in much French verse. That of the German I get hold of readily, and I am not deaf to the Italian. Russian, I don't know at all, probably because I know it only with my eye, not at all with my ear. Beljame of the Sorbonne was meaning to teach me the charm of Racine, but he died and left me in my ignorance. . . . I read all the good French books I can lay my hands on. I have seen but few from Germany, except, of course, the bulky apologies of the great men who shift the blame of their downfall to the other man's shoulders. They are a curious lot, and I see no signs of any regret for their evil deeds. I have heard of none, but then, after all, some of the English and

To Salomon Reinach

American pacifists proclaim that they are spotless. —I move to the country next week, to Hancock, New Hampshire; if you will send me a line at any time, that is my address. There, like Candide, I shall cultivate my garden. Voltaire is always right—that is why he is so hated—and never more so than now (as I told you *supra*) when all the cultivators of the soil have left it and run to the towns so that we are positively threatened with famine next winter; a pleasing prospect. . . .

Hancock, N. H., July 4. I am very much obliged to you for the *Revue Critique* and for *La Bossue d'Assise.* I love those papers of yours, which are as pleasant reading as madrigals, and yet are packed with learning and wisdom. Wisdom is a good sauce, it is of the essence of humour; that is to say, humour must express wisdom or it is nonsense. . . . I also saw J. de Pierrefeu on Stendhal, and I highly approve his opinion that Stendhal has been absurdly overpraised in these later years. It seems to me that the worship of him has been full of *snobisme*. One would think he had founded a religion, so devoted are his disciples to his relics. . . . I try hard to say nothing about things in this country. You can see the state of affairs as well as I can, and you will approve of it as much as I do. This is a bad world to live in, but we must put up with it as long as we are in it, and human life is short. . . .

Thomas Sergeant Perry

March 10, 1921. . . . What is going on here you know as well as I do, but you perhaps do not so well understand the black ignorance of the populace, its utter indifference to what is going on elsewhere. The German and Irish are forever at work denouncing the English and the French, and the pacifists are always making trouble. One of the curses of this country is that it puts all the power into the hands of inferior men. That is a result of democracy, which always means levelling *down*. Anything else savours of aristocracy and so is to be condemned. I have been filled with a certain sour amusement lately noticing the delight of certain newspapers in the fact that Harding is just a plain, common man, as if his incompetence were a virtue. I think that barring Russia this is the worst governed country in the civilised world—granting that we are civilised—not merely through its clumsy forms of government, but through the incompetence of its rulers and its absurd exaltations of democracy, etc. You see, I despair of the republic. Indeed I maintain that civilisation, this civilisation, is a wreck. It does not fall in one great crash like a circus tent, but a column falls here, another landmark there; the whole thing is crumbling. . . . It looks now as if Bolshevism were in some danger. If it doesn't fall this time it will another. Here it has had a fairly good press. It has been looked at by some so-called Intellectuals as an interesting social experiment, and its fall will be to them a cruel blow. Our old friend *The Nation*

To Salomon Reinach

has always had a good word for it, as it has had for pacifism and for the Germans. There is another red sheet, *The New Republic,* that worships Lenin and Trotsky and at times contains readable articles on books.—Have you seen W. James's letters? They are charming reading. He was a most interesting creature and is well presented in this book, without giving undue prominence to his philosophical work, of which I understand actually nothing; and those who are interested in philosophy seem to me to find in it only stuff to dispute about. No two of them agree. W. J.'s treatment of his colleagues is very entertaining. I knew him well, indeed from boyhood. . . . I have some faint hope that Harding may do something to help afflicted Europe. Our brutal indifference has been very painful to me. You will understand my comprehensive gloom. . . .

April 14. . . . The outlook for intellectuals is bad enough, but then perhaps there will be in a short time no intellectuals left to suffer. This country subsists without them. When the world gets completely upset something will be demanded of everyone that makes no great demand on the intellect. Thus do I croak every day. A friend of mine who shares my views, told me the other day that the only consolation he could find was that his father and grandfather wrote just such despairing wails at his age, which is mine. . . . As Renan said, "The stupidity of mankind was designed to give us a good notion of infinity."

Wasn't it Renan? I know the remark only at second hand, but I am very fond of it. . . .

May 15. It was only when a few days ago I received my French papers that I learned of the death of your brother. I send you my sincerest condolences. I had not the honour of his acquaintance, but I had seen him and, of course, knew his great importance, his boundless energy, his unending struggle for the right. What a family you are! One cannot speak of your brother without recalling Dreyfus. Did I ever tell you about my talk with ——? It was one day after dining . . . I happened to be sitting by the side of ——, and it came out that he had been in Paris during the Dreyfus time. I said, "You are just the man I have always wanted to meet, to put a few questions which, I'm afraid, you would find very indiscreet." He said, "Ask me anything you want," and I did. He knew all the incidents, about the bordereau, etc., and I asked him (with all apologies for my insistence, etc.) if he knew who wrote the paper. He did. "Was it D.?" "No, it was Esterhazy, he was our man."—I did not need this assurance to believe Dreyfus innocent. What convinced me of that was extracts from his letters published in the *Temps*. I felt and said everywhere that the man who wrote these letters was not a guilty man. You must excuse me if I have told you all this ancient history before.—I have received from a friend of mine the enclosed note about the electricity from the

To Salomon Reinach

ocean, and oddly enough I have seen in papers two vague references of late to the same problem. I suppose it is standing next in order for solution.— There are many problems not solved. I wish this country would cancel the French debt. We could do it, but the politicians find it an excellent excuse for all sorts of extravagance. . . .

June 27. . . . This poor clumsy country—another groping and sometimes grasping giant, stupid as most giants, is drifting, I hope, toward an honourable course, in spite of the politicians. . . . I have great respect for the judgment of the mass, as it comes out after all the eager minorities have made a noise that seemed to fill earth and heaven. It has shown itself in the general disgust with Harvey's speech and the general, very wide spread approval of Sims's speech. Still I am no enthusiastic admirer of democracy. It is the worship of words that fills this world with trouble, at least that is one important mischief-maker.. . .

August 15. . . . There seems to me to be no doubt that for a long time Wilson was unwilling to go into the war and dreamt of being the final arbitrator. They say he could not go in, that the strong sentiment of the West made it impossible, but this I doubt. . . . Cabot Lodge told me plainly that if the President had shown any tact the treaty would have gone through, but his obstinacy forbade. If he had asked the other senators to work with him, without gobbling all the glory, he would have done what he wanted to do and would have got glory enough. An envious disposition is the only vice that brings nothing but misery to its possessor. All the other defects have an alluring side, but the more envious you are, the worse you feel. It has no charm, like indolence, or drunkenness, or undue ambition. What the result of the discord is for the world I dread to think. Harding seems to be inclined to taking up the treaty, but those opposed to it are very strong. Lodge has a narrow vision, and is as obstinate as Wilson. The country at large has but the vaguest knowledge of the state of affairs in Europe, and is wrapt in the pettiness of life here. I feel very sad about it.—You speak of Roscoe Thayer's article. He is a worshipper of Roosevelt, and would kill Wilson slowly with his own hands. I am fond of him, though I am far from sharing his simple taste for the blood of his enemies. He can't help exaggerating. . . .

April 7, 1922. . . . It is in this way that America is prevented from being too powerful. *Le bon Dieu* sees to it that the trees do not grow too high and countries like Russia and the U. S. A. too mighty. Is it *le bon Dieu?* I have known agnostics and atheists, but I have never known anyone who doubted the existence of a personal devil. It must be he who directs us here. If you see in the papers that the French are becoming unpopular here, don't believe

To Salomon Reinach

it, for they are not, though the Germans would like everyone to think so. The country is becoming more and more indifferent to all the rest of the world, but to all alike in the whirl of present affairs.—The world is slow at getting together again, but think how long it was before it recovered from the Napoleonic wars, the Thirty Years War, etc. Here there are curious indications of possible Dark Ages. There is not only prohibition and a general movement threatened against tobacco, but also condemnation of any teaching of 'evolution, Darwinism or atheism'. The celebrated Bryan is out with a book against evolution, and I saw yesterday another, 'God—or Gorilla,' in which the gorilla has no chance. . . .

November 18. I am a wretched correspondent, but it is the knowledge of my errors that makes me merciful. I find that I can't write a letter that is not full of the gloomiest groanings over the state of the world. No raven ever croaked as I do whenever I take a pen in my hand, and the world outside is bad enough without further embittering from me. Hence, I don't write.—Especially now I am depressed by the indifference of this country to Europe. This indifference is due to gross ignorance and to the wicked talk of politicians. The country is so vast, so huge a bulk, that education enters it very slowly, and the way is blocked by a firm conviction that we are superior to every other land and need nothing from outside.—I have been reading the *Life* of Page

Thomas Sergeant Perry

(Ambassador to England) with the greatest interest. If you run across the book (two large and costly volumes—look at it and see how the poor man suffered in London as we did at home, from Wilson's detestable neutrality during the early part of the war. It was the most shocking period in our brief history, except perhaps the present. It is my opinion that Wilson prolonged the war more than any generals did. This *Life* is a most important document for the history of the war and ought to be put into French, as I dare say it will be. . . . I read in the *Temps* that at a meeting of the Institute, Mr. Reinach (S.) made a few remarks, and I sigh to know what they were. I am sure that our civilisation is going, but it is not wholly gone. There is practically none here to go. . . .

January 23, 1923. I enclose a letter written by a friend of mine after a long talk with me on the subject. I don't mean to imply that he was brought to these views by my powerful eloquence. Far from it, they were already formed, but in the talk they assumed their place and inspired him to jot them down. I find, too, that most of the thinking people, whom I meet, share those opinions. It may be that counting noses, you would find a majority thinking otherwise, but I am not sure. Certainly a great many deeply regret the position the country has taken about the debt and about the unwillingness to share or to try to lift the state of affairs. . . . Mr. [Moorfield]

To Salomon Reinach

Storey, who wrote the letter, is a lawyer of note, an ex-President of the American Bar Association, and an enthusiastic defender of all good causes. I have known and admired him for sixty years. He has never had any prominent public position. Those places are taken by men of very different calibre. A democracy hates above all things any form of superiority. . . . It was not I who sent you the Henry Adams book. I knew him well, and was at the table he speaks of at Cambridge with him. I don't wholly admire the book, and towards the end he gets beyond my understanding. It had wonderful success all over the country. I don't know why, unless that it started as something infinitely precious.—A more valuable book is the *Life and Letters of Page* of which I wrote to you. . . .

March 21. . . . To go back to your book (*History of Christianity*) : the main strength of the Church of Rome seems to me to be that it has a rule for every contingency, and thus is always ready to tell everyone what to do. The whole human race is sighing to be under some authority, to know how to have his hair cut, what height heels to wear. And the Catholic Church is willing to take the chair to assume that hardest duty, of giving orders. We like to talk about freedom, but we are naturally slaves. Critics tell us what books to read, what pictures to admire. As to the position towards the church of Brunetière, it is incomprehensible, but it is not necessary for me to write your book over again. It is a great book and I thank you for it.—I have received today Gorki's *Aufsätze die Zerstöring der Personlichkeit.* It looks like a good book. He points out the baleful effect of Tolstoi and Dostoievsky in the Russian character, though of course other things helped; the absence of independence, the vast power of all authority, the annihilation of all work in common. One thing played into the hands of another. Does a man become vain by looking into the glass? or does he look in because he is vain? Which is first, the hen or the egg? At all events, it is a comfort to find the names of Tolstoi and Dostoievsky mentioned in something not a mystical rapture. The English books about Dostoievsky are as exalted as his villains when they are most atrocious and at the same time close to the angels. I am very sure that I shall like this calmer book.

May 30. I received your most interesting and valuable letter some days ago, and on reflection I decided to send a copy of it to my friend Senator Lodge, the chairman of the Congressional Committee on Foreign Affairs. I said to myself that it could not fail to do them good. They are a wild lot, violently prejudiced, many of them, against taking any part in European affairs and apparently thinking they are as far from Europe as we are from Jupiter. Such are the ideas of Borah, Hiram Johnson, and Moses. Lodge is wiser, though we might neither of

To Salomon Reinach

us agree with all his views on this question. . . . Certainly the sympathy with France is growing all the time in this country, and I don't for my part come across much propaganda against that country. I do find, however, many men with whom I generally agree, strongly opposed to any part in straightening out the world. I can't understand this opposition, for after all, we are living in the same world and it is not a very large one as worlds go. . . . As I said, the Americans—the mass—do not know the French, and so do not envy them the possession of their distinctive qualities. As for the merits of the German, they are not envied by other people because no one wants more hard work, while one would like certain Gallic qualities and certain English ones, and would be the better for them. . . .

June 28. I have yours of the eleventh enclosing Senator Lodge's letter to me, and to him I have sent word of your and Poincaré's comments. I am very glad you let Poincaré see the letter, and I hope it did some good in showing what the chairman of the Committee on Foreign Affairs thought of matters. What is more important is, I take it, that Lodge should get the French view. The Senate is an ignorant, prejudiced body, reeking with domestic politics. The members (I mean the majority, not Lodge) know nothing of the rest of the world. They are mainly men who have failed in everything they have undertaken, and seek refuge in political life. I am not

Thomas Sergeant Perry

proud of what they have done and are meaning to do. . . . The Russian, the Moscow, Company came to this country and I saw them in *The Cherry Orchard* and in *The Three Sisters* of Chekhov. I had seen them in the first play in Petrograd in 1908. They were most impressive. Those plays were the most wonderful things I have seen on the stage; there is but one thing in my memory to compare with them —*Les Caprices de Marianne* in 1867 with Got, Delaunay, Bressant, Madeleine Brohan. That was perfection. I saw it twice with exquisite delight. Two or three times since then I have seen old birds recounting their rapture in that play in the *Temps*.— Yes, I know Croiset's *Greek Literature* very well. It seems to me far and away the best book on the subject. Pierre Loti of course I read, but I preferred the moments when he was not boasting of his successes. What extraordinary power of description he had; he was a landscape painter in words, a most difficult art; for think what shell-holes descriptions generally are, only to be avoided by the intelligent reader, but his are wonderful. . . . When one thinks of the oceans of ink consumed in descriptions that must be skipped one is reminded of the acres of canvas, a mass of *croûtes,* that tried to be landscapes. . . . I notice your remark about the approach of a time when the art of drawing shall have vanished. I share your gloom, partly perhaps on account of my advanced years, but more from what I see in the world. My friends and I meet, shake our frosty

To Salomon Reinach

polls, and croak all manner of dark prognostications. I am sorry this country so persistently makes itself detested. It holds an odious position, combining extreme selfishness with practical unwisdom. The country is so large, the mass is so great, that any change of opinion is very slow, but I am sure one will come. I hope not too late. . . . I think the people are slowly coming to the opinion that we live on the same planet with the Europeans. I judge so from scraps of talk with all sorts of people, and from my own firm opinion. I have found that whenever I have made up my mind about anything and feel disposed to plume myself on my lonely wisdom, two or three million other men had come to the same conclusion at least a week before. . . .

October 19, 1924. All these months I have thought of you very often, and at every turn in politics I have thought of a letter to you which should judge and condemn everything that happened, but you have been spared this infliction. Now we are in a political campaign, but I refuse to interest myself in it. I have decided how I shall vote and refuse to read anything about the matter in the newspapers. I have so often seen this tiresome contest when one half of the American people is trying to prove that all the other half are rascals that now I refuse to listen to them. They utter a half truth; they are all rascals.—The French, too, have this trial, and it certainly seems as if the whole human race had lost all intelligence, but

Thomas Sergeant Perry

I do not utterly despair. If the world has not enough sense to go right, it deserves to perish. Meanwhile there are some very interesting things to keep us occupied. I follow you in the meetings of the Academy of Inscriptions, etc. Is there no publication that gives a fuller report than the newspapers get? I saw your scepticism about the new Livy, an extraordinary incident. You spoke some time ago about the effort to make use of the tides for producing force. I see that this is near accomplishment at Brest. It has been tried more or less in this country and it was one of the many subjects investigated by Galton. Of course it will be made practicable. Indeed, I always say that there is nothing the human race wants which it does not get. . . . The papers say that men are about to let loose the force of an atom, and the consequence is that I am so convinced of the truth of my theory that I can't hear a door slam without thinking he has solved the puzzle and is blowing up the world. When I state this theory of mine and ask for one failure that will show its unsoundness, my opponents say that mankind has not yet abolished death, but then it is possible to remind them that while we may detest it for ourselves there may be others anxious to get into our shoes, so that there is a division of opinion. . . .

December 13. . . . André Beaunier always gives me great pleasure, and I should have given him my vote at the Academy the other day, if I had been

To Salomon Reinach

asked, rather than to Georges LeCompte. I read his three volumes on Joubert with much satisfaction. Then I am reading the letters of Madame du Deffand to H. Walpole (three massive 8vo vols., 750 pp., Methuen 1912). I am sure you will never read them. You are toiling on other things while I stroll in these pleasant paths. I remember thirty years ago John Fiske took down a volume of Voltaire's letters to look up something, and said: "I shall never read these letters, but you will"; and a few years later in Japan I found them lurking behind volumes of sermons on the shelves of an Archdeacon of the Church of England and I borrowed and read them. These letters of Mme. du Deffand, of course, contain much faded gossip, but they are full of bits one wants to read out loud. There are more than eight hundred letters, so I am contented for some time. . . . I hope the French debt will be arranged without undue brutality on our part. The Americans have not the art of presenting their side with grace. We are much tainted with barbarous ways. I follow your political and social troubles with an attentive eye. I must be now one of the older subscribers of the *Temps*, for I have read it steadily for nearly forty years. . . .

January 8, 1925. I received your most interesting letter of December 24, a day or two ago, and at once ran over to Cambridge to lay the letter of Claudius before Professor George F. Moore, who is the most learned man I know in America. He is professor of Comparative Religions at Harvard.—He was very much interested in your note and we agreed in thinking an hypothesis, a new one, a most fascinating thing. But, of course, it is like a bone thrown to the dogs; it creates great excitement, it is gnawed and tossed about, and then buried. Moved by the common instincts of humanity, we tore it to pieces; and it is these fragments that I now mean to lay before you. Moore wondered whether it was the communism of Christianity that was the characteristic mark at that time. It looks as if the current expectation was that the kingdom of heaven was to appear very soon, and then all the present conditions would be wiped away. Believing that, would even reformers make an attack on capital? We don't mend and paint a house that is to be torn down next week, and there would be no need of overthrowing a system that was sure to perish in a very few years.—Is not that the strangest objection to your suggestion? Moore had not seen Bell's book. Neither have I, but I shall look it up. I doubt if it has reached our libraries yet. I hope you are right, your suggestion would then throw much light on a dark period and on very obscure points. When I think of the general tolerance of the Romans for outlandish religions I should be surprised at this early outbreak, but I am a mass of ignorance. At any rate you have interested Moore and me greatly. . . .

To Salomon Reinach

January 16, 1926. . . . As for Robert Bacon, he was in no way an intellectual giant. He had every admirable quality, he was full of kindness, most amiable, generous and helpful. He was always good-natured, he was a beautiful object to look at, tall, well made, handsome, with a smile that would have melted the heart of a devil. . . . J. P. Morgan had a great fancy for being surrounded by handsome men, and took him into his firm, where he remained for a year or two and then went out with something like a million or so of dollars, as his share of the earnings. He went to Washington where he was indeed Secretary of State; and then, when the government wanted support, he was sent to talk to the recalcitrant, who was always brought into line by his delightful manners, his pleasant smile, and his lovely nature. I am sure that he had no more to do in the Harriman duel than you or I. All the time, he hated his life in finance. A friend of mine met him once at some Director's meeting or something of the kind, and Bacon said: "How I hate this business. If it were not for the need of making money, I should throw the whole thing over." My friend asked him what he would like to do. "Have perfect leisure and study music; try to do something in that." I knew him slightly, and always saw his charm, as everyone did. . . . As for the American philosophers, I think that when you have mentioned Emerson and James you have done all that was needed. . . . I used to make fun of William James, whom I knew well from 1858 till his death, about his philosophy. I should think Royce, a contemporary and friend of William James, was more important than Münsterberg, but my opinion is absolutely without value. . . . I saw Emerson several times, a *most* impressive man.

April 15. . . . This book (*The Book of Daniel Drew*) is apparently a dramatization of Daniel Drew's life. The facts are as he [the author, Bouck White] narrates them. They were notorious at the time, and are chronicled in *Chapters of Erie,* by Charles and Henry Adams, who would have been very glad to be sued for libel. I never saw Daniel or Jay Gould, but I did see Jim Fiske in the uniform of an English Admiral—think of it—seeing the steamboat off. Again I ran across him in a bus in New York, accompanied by two flashy women. I just missed his taking off. I had come from Philadelphia on my way to Cambridge and meant to spend a night with a friend of mine who lived near the hotel where I meant to take a room. The entrance, however, so swarmed with odious gamblers, etc., that I decided to go a few steps further, and so missed the slaughter which took place just when I should have seen it.—I find that the book when it appeared was warmly praised by serious journals. I thought I had seen an article in the *Nation,* but I can find none, but in the Annals of the American Academy of Political Science (I think) an approving review and in the

To Salomon Reinach

Journal of Political Economy, as well as elsewhere. Thus he is praised by I. M. Marcosson, a journalist who wanders all over the globe to interview kings and statesmen and then to write about them most intelligently. I mention these approvals to show how closely the author must have kept to the facts. The barbarous language is an attempt to show D. D.'s rustic speech. Marcosson writes in the *Saturday Evening Post,* a weekly journal with about a million subscribers. The "high-brow" generally sneers at it as merely the delight of the rabble, but I always defend it and often read it. . . . Apropos of the steamboat mentioned above, there were placed in it, near the staircase where everyone had to pass, a portrait of Jay Gould on one side, and of Jim Fiske on the other. Jim Fiske was showing them to Mr. Travers of New York who asked, "Yes, but where is the crucifix?". . .

December 11. . . . I am much struck by what you say of the way that French scholarship is going on, though the ranks of the workers have been so riddled and shattered. I was thinking of it the day before your letter came while on a longish motor ride, recalling the new names in the *Revue Critique.* I was thinking, too, of the insufficient laboratories in France and the narrowed incomes and rewards of research, and I wished I could get hold of one of our numerous millionaires, anxious, as many are, to do what is best with their money, that I might tell him some things. There was one man named Duke who

Thomas Sergeant Perry

made a vast fortune with tobacco—and wretchedly poor tobacco in my opinion. He meant to do his best and left sixty or eighty millions (dollars) to building and endowing a new university [1] in North Carolina. Here is a vast new plant, built with every comfort and convenience, but where can they find competent professors for this and the thousand other colleges and universities? Where competent students?—Another of my idle dreams—you see, I am one of those idlers who stand by the doors of the rich and great and determine how their money ought to be spent—is to catch a young man with plenty of money who has really nothing to do in this country except bore, or kill, himself with amusement, and start him at some archaeologic work. A few years ago I did run across in a railway trip to New York a young man reading Coptic. You can imagine my surprise and delight—not that I know more of Coptic than the shape of the letters. I fell on on his neck and found him interested in his work, but the war soon killed him. . . .

June 29, 1927. . . . I am much interested in what you tell me of the new edition of *Apollo,* and I shall turn at once to your pages on the new schools, or kindergartens, that have of late done so much more in the way of talking than of painting. I am a hopeless conservative who maintains that one duty of art

---
[1] Duke University, including Trinity College, and the old buildings, at Durham, North Carolina.

To Salomon Reinach

is to give pleasure, and that affectation does not give pleasure to the beholder—but I won't go on, I wait to see how you tackle the problem. It is amusing to live long enough to hear the condemnation of the immediate past which seems the main duty of every new generation. In Victorian days we spoke ill of the eighteenth century, now it is the nineteenth that is in ill favor. In time there will be condemnation of even the Georgian period. . . . It is everyone's day dream, the spending of other peoples' money. Just now there is a movement in this country to establish a University that shall teach the young all the principles of fundamentalism and the literal truth of every word in Holy Writ. In which the world is as amusing as ever, and perhaps the most amusing are those who imagine it will ever be anything but this strange mixture of facts and fancies that surround us. . . .

July 21. I have been improving my mind by reading the compressed and abbreviated one volume *Golden Bough*—the Golden Twig it might be called—and I confess with more illumination to my mind than the whole twelve volumes gave me, for my judgment then was overwhelmed by the mass of details. I couldn't see the wood for the trees. Do you know this volume? The process of condensation has been admirably done. Reading it and at the same time running over Isaac Taylor's *Origin of the Aryans,* I have seen what an amount of light Frazer has thrown on these investigations. Taylor's book, 1890, is, it seems to me at least, a good handbook, but he halts or stumbles over things that Frazer has made very clear.—It is odd how many old beliefs still linger. Priests and men in high places would be driven away, generally killed, if the weather was hopelessly bad. In this country a bad season for agriculture before an important election is always dreaded by the party in power, they are sure to be driven out by an enraged public. Politicians are now beginning to worry about the crops this year, when next year a President is to be chosen.—Then in private life I am continually struck by the way trees are esteemed. Cutting one down is in the general opinion, not of farmers but of people from the cities, only a modified form of murder. This feeling of respect is all that is left of what once was worship. Other duties have known this diminution. . . .

December 1. . . . I have been made very happy by seeing that what was no more than a happy vision about help to the languishing schools of France has come true at least in the matter of the work at Lyon, to which the younger Rockefeller has given a good sum. The old gentleman occasionally gives a child a ten-cent piece, but the younger one has done most noble work in many directions. Wasn't it Herodes Atticus who set the fashion in Greece? This man is another, and it's sad to see how little credit he gets for it. Everyone feels envy, and no one admiration.

To Salomon Reinach

I have seen no comment in the papers on this last deed of kindness.—I have spent the summer in the country very idly, though I have read more or less M. Juret's Latin Syntax among other things. Gourmont's most touching *Lettres Intimes,* and have now before me Pierre Villey's *Marot and Rabelais,* which I find delightful, most agreeably instructive. I spoke to you before about Ernst Ludwig's *Napoleon* and *Kaiser William II.* There is a new volume, the Bismarck, good but less interesting. What the book does show very plainly is the attitude of the German mind to an official, to one who commands. The huge book is worth reading to see that. , . .

VIII

(To Joseph C. Grew)[1]

Hancock, N. H., August 21, 1917. Dear Joe: . . . There is no news here. Mr. Hoover would be delighted to see our vegetable gardens, Edith's, Alice's and our own. Like most cultivators of the soil, we leap from fear of flood to dread of drouth, or drought, as you prefer. I see that Mr. Egan is in trouble with his health and very possibly, I suppose, will be unable to work again. I wonder what deserving Democrat will succeed him. Really, when I hear them all say this is a war for democracy, my heart does not leap in my bosom. Democracy is just as unsatisfactory as anything else. It happens merely that autocracy has made an unusually bad showing and so the opposite failing is admired. In time we shall all be shouting for an intelligent autocracy. . . .

Boston, April 9, 1920. Have you seen Cardinal Mercier's Own Story? It is a wonderful book and it brands the Germans for all time. It is made up of the letters between the Cardinal and the German officials, with a mere meagre statement of the inci-

---

[1] As Mr. Perry's letters to his son-in-law, Joseph C. Grew, now United States Ambassador to Turkey, were obviously never intended for publication, only a few selections have been chosen for this volume.

To Joseph C. Grew

dents that called for the letters. The fencing is the prettiest thing in the world, the Cardinal's courtesy is perfect—when he makes a mistake, he calls *touché* and salutes and is ready for the next go—but when he is angry, his courtesy remains, but his fury is magnificent. I assure you, Joe, it is a *great* book, one of the few great ones of the world. Do get it and study it. If you haven't it already, get the *Journal d'une Comédienne Française sous le Terreur Bolchevik, par* Paulette Pax. It is a capital picture of the Bolshevik brutes and will interest you who know Petrograd. It has real value as a document. . . .

June 24. Your beauteous photograph arrived yesterday, and I hasten to express the joy it gave and gives us. To be sure, you look rather tired and a bit thin, but Alice says one gets fat in Denmark, and we recall Hamlet's figure and so are comforted. . . . Your new clothes are also immortalised. I gaze at them, too, with rapture. I could chat for a long time about your motor trip.[1] Sindbad's various voyages seem dull in comparison. I am sure that the swiftness of your run, combined with the elegance of your new English clothes, will give you a place in Danish mythology, alongside of Osric and Hamlet. You will be said to have come on a flash of lightning, or on wings. Poems will be written about you, and future ages will wonder whether you really ever existed or

---
[1] From Paris to Copenhagen, when Mr. Grew was appointed Minister to Denmark.

were only a sun myth. There will be many strong arguments for this hypothesis. This god-like creature flashed through Denmark of a summer's day, at the very beginning of June, when the sun is most potent and is highest in the heaven. When it was nearly setting there arrived before the palace the sun god himself, whom tradition says shone in beautiful armour (your English clothes). No such speed was ever known, it outstript that of railway trains. He entered one of the buildings and there was no one who dared to wait upon him,[1] but he took the things himself, thus illustrating the fertilising force of Helios. Yes, one could write a very forcible pamphlet about this theory. It must have been most interesting to see Berlin. Even the week after being kicked out of a place, you like to go back to it as victors and to be once more at the Embassy! Yes, it must have been interesting. Those dramatic corners in life count. . . . The other day L. went to the studio, opened the door and left the key outside, shut it and found herself immured, almost entombed, Ginevra-like, in that vault. Her screams were useless. We didn't miss her, and never would have looked for her there. We shudder to think what might have been her end, but she opened a south window and escaped. . . .

July 8. . . . You say what must be often im-

[1] Referring to a strike of waiters in the hotels. The family were obliged to serve themselves.

To Joseph C. Grew

pressed upon you, that Copenhagen is a small place. I have seen the diplomatic life of Tokyo, and have had experiences to prove the morbid interest that follows the foreigner in a small place and the exact knowledge it acquires. Once in Tokyo I received from a French missionary a bill for some French bread that he used to supply, with a note asking for early payment if convenient, "as it probably would be, because I had just received a new letter of credit." How did he know that? I had sent for and got the new letter, but of course had said no more about it than if I had got a new cheque book, and one enriches you as much as the other. I asked him where he got his information, but there was no answer. Some Jap at the bank must have told him. Look out for your digestion next winter when the dinner campaign opens. The tennis club will be delightful and you will find some good players. I wonder if they have in-door courts? And is it the Hellerup Club? What you tell me of the Soviets and their efforts to get into business, and of the strike, is most interesting. I don't see where Denmark is to get coal, and without coal everything must stop. It has no water power of course, so manufactures must suffer. In Norway and Italy water power can be developed, but where you are? You will see some very pretty problems unfolding themselves before you, and I wish our country could profit from them. You will see Cox has been put up against Harding, six of one, half a dozen of another, except that Cox seems to me much the brighter of the two. The newspapers talk of W. W. taking the stump. No such miracle since Lazarus. I regret the position of the Republican senate about the League, but I think half the fault is W. W. for his obstinacy in throwing down every modification of his plan. May not Grey have been sent away because he ventured to suggest compromise? About ——, I have no confidence in him. . . . I don't know him, but I know his kind, pacific in wartime, warlike in peace, and always pro-German and pro-Bolshevik. But of course you are not free to say these things. Egan's book I can well understand should appear indiscreet—it was indiscreet. It is very hard to talk about a lot of living people in a way to please them all. . . . Outsiders just love an indiscreet writer. One always yearns to see the passages cut out. Egan must be a good fellow in spite of his book. . . .

July 24. Here there is no more news than in Copenhagen—not so much. . . . As for Cox and Harding, they are a pair. They bring out pro-German articles from Cox's paper and idiotic sentences to match from Harding's speeches in the Senate, where among other gems he said: "I am hesitant to say." The idea of voting for a man capable of that is very repellant, but I suppose I shall come to it. One can't uphold the Democrats, they have shown their incompetence in finance, in almost every direction. M. Storey means to vote their ticket, through devotion to the League, but I shall ask him how he

To Joseph C. Grew

can vote for a party that so treats the negro. And how we Americans treat them! We make a lot of talk about the war to make them free, and they are snubbed, crushed, despised and maltreated as if lower than slaves. Apart from the unkindness to a fellow-being, think of the unwisdom of cultivating millions of enemies in your country. . . . More interesting, yet not wholly unlike, are the yacht races, the drifting matches, in the windless landlocked bay of New York. I hope Lipton will get the cup. If he gets it, there is a chance that the sport, so terribly emasculated here, may revive on the English coast with real boats in a real wind on a rough sea. That is the only yachting that is of any use. It is not a drawing room game for safe harbours with guaranteed gentle zephyrs; it's a man's sport, at least it should be, and they will make it so. I am sick of this ladylike racing. Long Island Sound is responsible for much of the super-refinement of modern American yachting. New York millionaires built themselves villas on its shores and found they could build boats with huge mainsails and no end of jibs which would have been impossible when the wind blew, and for amusement they skimmed the north surface of the Sound. . . .

January 27, 1921. . . . Before I go further I must send you the opening lines of an article on John Slidell in the same review (*American Historical,* Jan. 21, p. 255). "In John Slidell the confederacy

Thomas Sergeant Perry

possessed its ablest diplomatic agent. Born in New York in 1793 of a family on marriage terms with some of the most distinguished of Northern leaders, including Commodore Perry of Lake Erie fame, Slidell had linked his entire personal and political fortunes with the Lower South." I thought that you, being also "on marriage terms" with that noble family, might be interested. Was ever such English? . . . How about giving me a berth as translator to your legation? Salary not so much an object as a steady home. . . .

June 18. Before I forget it, let me call your attention to what must be a most enchanting book, noticed in *Times* Literary Supplement (of London, of course) of June 2. It is *Sport in Asia and Africa,* by Sir Richard Dane. (Melrose, '21). The account of it makes me want to take my airgun, or better, my shotgun, down to Juggernaut (a pond in Hancock) and wait for a chance to shoot a rhinoceros. I know you will like the book. Other than this advice I have little to say. . . . By the way, I notice you faithfully read to children the *Tales of a Wayside Inn,* but I ask myself is it really worth while to spend much time on such diluted literature as the amiable Longfellow provides? I know it is the custom in this country in order to Americanize the children's minds. I have seen the readers given to your children, containing an abundance of newspaper poetry of no value, or, worse than that, stuff that will

To Joseph C. Grew

forever sicken children with literature. Before this outbreak of patriotism children were brought up on bits of real literature—extracts from Shakespeare, Byron, Shelley, Wordsworth, are what I distinctly recall—I was talking about those Readers last Sunday with Robinson—and they burned into my memory. Those are the things the children should be introduced to if you want their lives enriched. Longfellow was a good man, but, except very rarely, an ordinary poet. Give the young things the real stuff, and their taste once formed, they will be able to choose for themselves. Roman children were not brought up on Ennius, but on Greek literature. You can't feed an active mind on the juiceless straw of Bryant and Whittier. You see the results of such poor fare in the sort of verse the *Transcript* readers ask for every Saturday evening. I feel very strongly about this, and I hope that the *Ersatz* will be thrown away. Read them the *Golden Treasury,* the *Oxford Book of Verse* and let Daddy Longfellow have a rest. I hope I don't seem to be ordering you about, for that I am unwilling to do, but I am anxious to urge my words upon you; and by the way, if you approve of them and lack the *Oxford Book of English Verse,* get one printed on India paper. It is much less cumbersome. . . .

June 22. . . . Overcome with emotion I stopped there. Now I go on, and since I seem to see you foaming at the mouth and tramping up and down your gallery, swearing at me for presuming to dictate how you shall bring up your children, Alice in tears on the sofa, and all the children wailing because they can't have the collected works of Mrs. Sigourney, I withdraw so far as to say that if you must administer American classics, the *Wayside Tales* will do very well, but in general the movement towards cramming American literature down [?] is more patriotism (of a parochial kind) than love of belles-lettres. So forgive me! . . .

July 24. I wish you could see this house. Accustomed as you are to royal palaces and princely castles, you would stop to say you had never in effete Europe seen anything like this. The whole mansion has been painted of a blazing white, and the blinds of a deep green, rivalling the sapphire or ruby, or whatever the stone is—emerald of course. The gifted brush of Lester Johnson has wrought this wonder. . . . To my grief—— fell out of the tournament a day or two ago. He simply went to pieces. I wish I could have had the good fortune of playing with him some time when, if he managed to hit the ball, he was sure to knock it into the net or out of bounds. Given those conditions, with ordinary luck, I should have beaten him. And how proud you would have been of your poor old pa-in-law. You would never have dared play with me yourself, and you would have recounted to all the courts, royal and tennis, in Europe, the old man's prowess: "He isn't much now, except of course

To Joseph C. Grew

to look at, but only a few years ago he beat —— out of his boots. And the best thing is how modest he is about it. He always says he expected —— to beat him, and probably another time the game would come out just the other way." What happened yesterday in the athletic conflict I don't know and don't very much care. I noticed that the English fellows laugh at our rigid training and no smoking. I remember when the crew were worked hard and then forbidden to assuage their thirst. They used to carry pebbles in the mouth, like Demosthenes, to relieve the dreadful drought. . . . By the way, when is the Sovietic government going to break down in Russia? We have been liberally fed with prophecies of the impending smash, but nothing happens except a further accumulation of horrors. S. Reinach tells me he has been seeing people just out of Russia, and their stories are most terrible, but they seem not to mind it, at least to do nothing about it. Still, as he says, Russian hours are long. . . .

August 24. As all the courts of Europe know, this is Old Home Day, and I trust the Legation flag is flying in our honor. I need not say that Hancock is celebrating the occasion with all its usual thoroughness. There are running races, swimming contests, baseball games; later, fireworks and a dance. At two there is speaking on the part of invited guests. Vice-President C. Coolidge, Sen. Moses, and B. L. Young (Harvard '07), speaker of Mass. House. That is at

Thomas Sergeant Perry

least the list of *invited* orators. How many are coming I don't know. . . . If I had been of the Committee I should have made an even more imposing list of *invited* guests, thus: President Harding and De Valera, Messrs. Lloyd George, Clemenceau, Lenin, Trotzky, King Christian X, Kerensky, Bela Kun, Chas. Eliot, Sen. Harrison, etc., etc.—*invited* guarantees nothing. And by the way, you can thank high Heaven that you are not here, for you would have had to get up on the stage to recite your little piece, and you might not have cared to make further oratorical efforts. I shouldn't have minded it so much, because I should have sat in a front seat and have made faces at you, as I did at the Commodore Perry celebration at Newport a few years ago. My old schoolmate, Senator George P. Wetmore was in full blast over the Commodore's glory when he caught my eye and it slowly winked at him, as in our happy boyhood, and he smiled but soon calmed himself. I can't think that any normal man can ever want to make a speech. Although I hate to pain a budding orator, I can't readily see why anyone should want to listen to one, for this reason: the orator seldom speaks from an overflowing heart, from an irresistible desire to say something but generally to get through a half hour of enforced entertainment of others. He is performing a conventional social duty. I was just wondering to John Morse why it was that the populace call for a speech as the one thing needed to make the bliss of this world complete. It is a great

To Joseph C. Grew

puzzle, and I must try to think it out while the invited speakers are at work. Perhaps the world will grow away from speechmaking after all. There was a time when people actually enjoyed sermons. It is to be remembered, however, that then sermons were almost the only lofty intellectual entertainment, and there was not too much of the commonplace; the sermons, too, were often clever and amusing, full of wit and eloquence. I assure you they are not bad reading, are *good* reading indeed. I seldom ran after a sermon, even of the kind I praise, but when I meet them I like to read perhaps one—seldom more at a time. They are better than many novels. I must not go on or I shall be crushing the young Demosthenes in you. . . .

August 25. As the date implies, our great function is over. . . . There was much painful music, a brass band that almost blew the roof off. Coolidge and Sen. Moses did not appear. . . . One funny thing is this: There was sitting on the platform yesterday, when we went in, a man all in white (Palm Beach raiment)—white shoes and stockings, tall and rather fine looking. Naturally I thought it was Senator Moses, who had come on from Washington in the usual attire of that torrid (or that horrid) city, and looking at him I thought he might have something to say, but when he rose and began to pray aloud I was puzzled. It was well for the founder of the family to come down from the mountain with the laws, but for this one to come up to them—I couldn't understand it till I found this holiday attire decked the village parson, the Reverend W. Pitkin, and that the real Moses was, to be sure, motoring through the state with a half promise to get here if he could. The same was true of the Vice President. . . .

August 28. . . . By the way, if you pass by the road along the southern shore of Lake Garda, don't fail to turn at the mile post turn, only eight kiloms., to see the peninsula of Sirmione. It's a beautiful spot, with the Scaliger castle and the Roman ruins, said to be of Catullus's villa. Catullus at any rate wrote about the spot (XXXI) *"Paeninsularum, Sirmio, insularumque Ocelli."* Years ago I saw it, going by train from Milan to Verona and wanted to clamber out of the wagon to visit it, and often passed it with regret, finally making up my mind I should never see it. Imagine then my joy at stumbling on the sign post when bicycling with L. and M. from Verona to Desenzano! Don't eat any meal at Peschiera. If you get to Vicenza, try to get trout served to you. . . .

November 3. . . . The men are at work installing the new furnace. It has a portentous crater, directly over the furnace, rather more I should think than a yard in diameter. The inner circle is to pour forth heat, while all round it sinks the cold air to be heated and issue again, in accordance with familiar laws of

To Joseph C. Grew

nature. In fact, however, I have lost much of my confidence in the laws of nature. Text-books have overdone their praise. They are like all laws, made to be broken. We found in our waterworks that the water simply refused to run down hill. Within the house, the water at times refuses to heat. You will see then that I very naturally hesitate to praise the furnace too warmly. I am afraid of being warmer than the furnace, but we shall see. This huge crater, reminding me of Asamayama, yawns in the dining room just before the yellow sofa which you remember. . . . Later. The new furnace is tremendous. It is like having your house heated by a private volcano. It sends forth heat, not in volumes, but in whole libraries. Not since my last Turkish bath have I known such fury. It would remind you of your summers at Cairo. It races and tears through the whole house, except the rooms which are protected with doors. Hancock's severest winters would be powerless against it. Tomorrow we shall keep it barely going. The cards of your trip were most welcome.[1] It must have been delightful. Hanover I saw once when Tiffany went from Cologne to Göttingen to see Charley Grinnell and got caught in the tail of the Prussian army in the '66 war and had to go to Hanover for a few hours. We were at the same hotel with the then King Wilhelm—the grandfather—and Bismarck. Zürich I know. . . .

[1] Motor trip from Copenhagen to Berne, through Germany, when Mr. Grew was appointed Minister to Switzerland.

Thomas Sergeant Perry

Boston, December 1. . . . The weather appears to be that of winter. The long storm that raged when I last wrote, has at last given way, and yesterday was clear. The loss of trees is enormous and the country is said to look like devastated France. The snapping of the branches during the nights is said to have closely resembled the noise of shell fire. I told you we just got in as the storm was beginning. Bill Hanson got back, with some difficulty after Wilton, at 10:15 P.M. and says there is a fall of snow on the ground there and that is useful for hunting the deer. . . . The storm here was the most disastrous ever known. Yesterday I was at M. Storey's and heard the account of the devastation wrought at Lincoln, which, as I told you of other cases, reminds veterans of France. Almost all his trees were completely ruined. Apparently it will take years to repair the damages, for in one night nature can undo the work of a long lifetime. It is really something dreadful. Curiously enough this same storm coming off the Pacific, hit Oregon and Washington very hard, doing no end of damage to the fruit trees. I suppose the Japanese prepared it. No disarmament conference can protect us from nature's malice. The seashore here was not hurt. The ocean doesn't seem now at this season to be very balmy, but it was balmy enough. The sacking of the hotels in Vienna is a piece of bad news. It is one of the signs of the revolutions threatening pretty much all Europe and elsewhere. Our civilization is simply crumbling; every now and

To Joseph C. Grew

then a good bit falls with more or less of a crash and then for a time there is quiet, as the other night when the branches were snapping from the trees overburdened with ice. Did you ever read *My Second Country,* by Robert Dell (Lane, 1920)? It is full of most accurate description of the French people—perhaps bearing on when he mentions their faults—and most gloomy prognostications about their future and the general future of Europe. He himself is above all things a Socialist. Socialism, he thinks, is inevitable and most desirable, although he makes out a list of the damage that socialism might do, which reads like a list of prizes. I think the book would interest you, as well as depress you. It's not merely rheumatism that inspires my gloomy words. They express my deliberate opinion when I am not tortured. . . .

December 29. . . . It is rash of me to start on another sheet, but I see no place on the other for the expression of my respectful homage to Your Excellency. You must like being called by that name as much as I liked being called Professor. It always sickened me, but you must get it now and then. It is necessary to be a German to get all the delight that is to be derived from that one word. . . .

May 14, 1923. . . . Since I wrote I have been to a movie, over-persuaded by Jim McLane, who assured me it was worth seeing, but it was not. The amusing part was a man's climbing up the outside of a 10- or 15-story building, with all sorts of ridiculous incidents as if about to fall, etc., etc., but the whole thing was poisoned by an underplot of "love" for the most odious and most idiotic girl that you can imagine. I said to J. McL. that I wished the woman in front of me had put on her hat to hide the whole stage from me, for it was common, repulsive beyond belief. I shall never go again to a movie play. I had been only once before, with Howells. It was also ghastly in its silliness. It is that form of amusement that is crowding out real acting. But I won't preach. Lausanne seems to be acquiring some of the liveliness of a town in the Far West before that part of the world was suffering under a burden of pseudo-civilization.[1] I hope you carry what your fellow countrymen call a "gun", by which I believe they mean a pistol. The glorious reputation of the U. S. A. for swiftness on the trigger and deadliness of aim ought to enable you to put through any of the diplomatic stunts assigned to you. I hope you have already practised shooting from the pocket. It is ruinous to the clothes but fatal to the foe. A grateful fatherland will, after years of postponement, give you another suit, but made in this country, with puffs on the shoulders, peg-top trousers and scanty pockets. . . .

[1] A member of the Soviet Delegation had been murdered during the Conference of Lausanne.

To Joseph C. Grew

Newport: May 30, 1923. . . . There is nothing particular to tell you of Newport. It looks very charming in spite of the cold. Now when it is not littered up by millionaires, it is delightful. Later, they spoil every prospect. It is curious to see their mansions on every rock, commanding a view into their neighbours' backyards and exposing their own. They have no need of a radio to hear what others are saying, they can "listen in" at no expense at all. They share the privilege which it was supposed had been confined to tenements. This is true democracy. . . .

Hancock, June 18. . . . I don't wonder Americans desire not to touch the European questions. There are so many of them and they are so contradictory. Any attempt at devising a solution, generally so easy when we consider our neighbour's affairs, in their case becomes so difficult as to be impossible. One gives up any attempt at suggestion. Yet, of course, these complications make some effort necessary. I was glad to read Col. House's sensible article. . . . I don't go to Cambridge for commencement, though I haven't my usual excuse—the hot weather. It's a nuisance taking the trip in the hot, dirty train, and one's pleasures after getting there are most moderate. I find myself in a crowd of strangers, and generally utter a loud scream and rush from the place. I cannot regard it as a pleasant occasion. Even the honour of walking near the head of the procession does not tempt me. You are well out of it. May fortune smile on, not at, your conference. You are doing your part to pacify the world, but what a world it is! . . .

June 26. You have been so kind in telling me what could be known about certain points of your professional life that I have a real sympathy with you, beginning an important and difficult career. I feel that I can encourage you with my advice, and more than that, can guide you with my example, till in time you rise to that super-diplomacy in which men like Bismarck and Metternich and me are accustomed to work. It may interest you to see how we work; it may inspire you with new zeal to see what are the threads weaving the fate of the world and how they are controlled, with what wisdom and tact. . . . What I haven't told you, though I'm sure it will interest you as a lover of large game, is the way our man freed the countryside from a monster that had been devastating the whole region. We were all in terror. Our crops were so intimidated that they didn't dare to have their heads above the ground. Not one of us thought of going out after dark. You of course will guess a tiger. I almost hear one of the children whispering *skunk*. No, it was the ravenous woodchuck. He was shot and we all sang the appropriate hymn: "How much wood would a wood chuck chuck, if a wood chuck could chuck wood?" Not content with that, we ate him,

To Joseph C. Grew

delicately cooked, and he was delicious, like a superior chicken. Did you eat your tiger? Try the next one you shoot. . . .

August 27. Hancock has been permeated with social events since I last wrote. L. and M. went over to the Franklin MacVeagh's to hear Gen. Allen talk on the state of Europe and our duty. I stayed at home. . . . Then Sunday, yesterday, Mr. Franklin MacVeagh, Jim and Francis came over to lunch. Mr. MacV. is a man 85 years old, but wonderfully spry and jolly. L. invited him over and he was willing to come. We had a pleasant lunch and he sat till 4 (also went to studio) when he had to go back to meet some people who had threatened to come to take tea with him. . . .

August 28. I told you, I hope in the interest of justice, that our excellent cook also won a first prize [1] for the rolls she sent in. She should have had a gold medal. No particular news. Our, or rather Alice's Aunt Susan Cabot, who is at Dublin, is coming over to lunch with us. The Fords moved in yesterday. I am rather amused by Breckenridge's fury with Lord Birkenhead's remarks about W. W. The fact is we boast of our freedom of speech, but get into a rage if anyone else exercises it in criticism, or even comment, of us. We feel free to hand our advice or reproof to anyone, but if anyone dares to talk to us in that way,

[1] At the County Fair.

the nation is indignant. It's just the way that we take it to be the natural and proper thing that all foreigners should seek American citizenship, but when H. James became an English citizen, it aroused fury. It seemed a crime. . . . Every Englishman knows our supersensitiveness, though I do think it is wearing off. It's not as bad as it was, and at times it has been almost justified by things said, though always it would be better not to notice them. Even Dickens scarcely exaggerated. Then, too, how unwise to show you are stung! In this case, Lord B. seems to me absolutely in the right, and I think our Bar Association will hold that view. M. Storey is going to their meeting at Minneapolis, or I should write to him to learn his views. I rather think Breckenridge, from mistaken loyalty, slopped over. Criticism of W. W. is not blasphemy.—In this country freedom is inclined to mean freedom to prevent another man from saying what he wants to say and doing what he wants to do. Of course such repression is a natural human instinct, more or less. We are beginning to learn it. I notice that the Dry Congress in Copenhagen is opening an attack on tobacco. Of course it was a matter of common knowledge that this was coming. It will be a long fight and I am safe from molestation. . . . In Kansas there is already a law or project of law forbidding the use of tea. Safety first! When we are all brought down to birdseed and pap we shall be the greatest people that ever lived. . . . The Russian company is coming

To Joseph C. Grew

again this winter, of course, because this country is for them a perfect gold mine. I told you I saw *The Cherry Orchard,* which you, Scott and I saw the first spring I was in Petrograd, and practically the same company. I was amazed that I remembered it so well, but it had made a tremendous impression on me. I shall see *The Three Sisters* again. I had read it several times, but had formed no idea of how pathetic it was on the stage. It is a great play. . . .

November 14. . . . I am reading at the same time the life of another eminent diplomat, Bismarck. You, too, will enjoy it if you ever get an evening to read it. It will take more than one evening to get the whole, for it is a bulky volume which you will *greatly* enjoy, as I said, and in many ways. I used to see the old fellow in Berlin 60 years ago. I don't mean that I met him, but *saw* him from afar. He was an impressive creature and looked just like his photographs. Ludwig has done admirable work in making modern Germany intelligible to the rest of the world. I never before understood the complicated state of affairs there in the 60's, before the war with Austria. I was there just after the war and read the papers, but the German knows better than anything how to make everything obscure, and by the Germans I don't mean Ludwig. . . . At the barber's yesterday, they had the radio turned on and it seemed to me as if I could hear the crumbling of civilization in the hideous chatter of the comic man and the sickening music. I think the radio is a curse to humanity in its lighter moments. However, I won't go on grumbling. You will see how my loneliness depresses me, and that my despondency is easily explained by my solitude.

January 1, 1926. You advise me to take up golf but, my dear fellow, I am an old golfer. 25 yrs. ago John Morse and I used to play on the Warren Farm course. There was only one man I could beat and in one of my absences from the country he died (probably from a broken heart) and when I got back no one could play with me. Now it is too late, all the sands of life have settled in my right hand and wrist so that I couldn't swing a club without anguish. Anyway I infinitely prefer tennis as the nobler game.

April 7, 1926. Don't let this alarmingly prompt letter disturb you. I demand no answer, I simply write to thank you for yours of the 8th and to send to the Dep't. my congratulations over the Chili-Peru truce and my prayers for the Lausanne treaty. I saw that 131 bishops (Episc. I regretted to see) reared on end against it. I take it for granted they know very little about the question, and I sometimes wonder how they would treat suggestions from the Dep't. of State with regard to their conventions. I cannot see what good the Armenians would get from tearing up the treaty, and to give the Turks more reason for

To Joseph C. Grew

disliking us seems superfluous. We are hated by enough people now, and hate is never of any use to a country—I mean of course being hated. I often see and read as much as I can stand of the Cong. Record. I sometimes ask myself if there is any corporate body in the world for which I have less respect than I feel for our Senate.

There is a book, *Choses d'Allemagne, par* A. Dumaine (1925) which I think might entertain you and A. Dumaine you may know. He was (wasn't he?) the last French Ambassador in Vienna and had long been in Germany. You will find mention of many of your old friends, and the book is distinctly entertaining.

I frankly say—(I am frank to say! to use the customary phrase) though the confession is very mortifying—that I feel for once unable to give any directions to the State Dep't. about Chili and Peru. I must let it go as you decide. I have no views on the rights of the case. I don't believe there are any rights. It is an odd thing, but I don't feel perfectly sure that I have a clear idea about the state of affairs in China, the names of the warring generals I find very confusing, and I abstain—to the detriment of national prosperity—from giving you the usual wealth of advice. You will miss it, but you must do the best you can. If America were only as insulated and isolated as she is said to be, I would gladly give you a shove, but I never can remember which is Chang and which Whang.

Thomas Sergeant Perry

April 14, 1926. F. . . . has sent me the tobacco and I beg you to accept my warmest thanks. Politeness urges me to tell you that I find it delicious, but when I reflect that this letter is to go to Washington [1] where the great G. W.'s example of honesty at any cost is never forgotten, I hesitate to perjure myself even if I break your heart by telling you that I don't like it. It is avowedly aromatic, so is the goat, the skunk, its near neighbour, the skunk cabbage. I think D. F. (O, suggestive initials!) put too much of his wife's perfume into the 'baccy.

You will never forgive my ungrateful heart and pen. You will say: "Could he never learn the first principles of diplomacy? not hide his agony under a polite smile?" I am sorry thus to shatter the ideal you had formed of me, but so it is. I am lost to sense of shame.

Farewell. I am sure you will never write again unless it be to send a venomous note telling me with what loathing you took one sufficient puff of my tobacco, a combination of asafetida and poison gas. . . .

June 25. While Mr. K. is away, getting his best silver out of the vaults to let it shine before the Prince, the country feels safe; insurance falls; stocks rise; warm weather at last appears; man and nature rejoice, and I take again my pen to thank you for letting me see that very interesting report on Russia.

[1] At this time Mr. Grew was Under Secretary of State.

To Joseph C. Grew

It really looks as if those fellows had begun to get a faint glimpse of the fact that a custom existing all over the world since time was, might prove as genuine as a theoretic system devised after reading a book. Savages began with barter and adopted paying in cash; the Russians seem to be learning to do the same thing. I think the writer of the report was perhaps overglad to hear expressions of the love of America. One always loves the man who is going to lend him a lot of money—until he asks for it back. He seems to be an intelligent creature and to have talked well to the many Russians he met. . . . How delightful of the Russians to feel "insulted" by Hughes's note! They must get used to such blows. Washington is in its usual messy state. In my opinion the attack on Coolidge by pushing the Farm bill will only hurt the pushers. I fear they will find themselves in a hole. What a filthy business politics is! We see the politicians painting themselves for this attack and are supposed to think they are in earnest. I don't wonder there are anarchists. The Cong. Record, if only anybody read it, would spread misery and discontent throughout the land.

Yesterday was Commencement. I did not go to taste its joys, tho' it was my 60th year out. I told them at my 50th not to expect me till the 100th. . . .

August 28, 1926. You have charge, I believe, for a few days; your duty is very clear: support the market and crush big business; thwart Wall St. in every way and keep everyone occupied. Make the farmer contented with what he earns and keep prices as low as you can. By observing these simple rules you will make everyone happy and win unending glory, if there is such a thing.

Nov. 5, 1926. D. so far forgot himself as to say "I am frank to say." If ever you catch the disease prevalent in Washington and say those words, I shall suffer acutely. I think W. W. used the phrase, but am not sure. You ought to send a copy of Fowler's *Modern English Usage* to every consulate, legation, and embassy.

Boston, April 17, 1928.[1] I didn't finish this wretched scrawl yesterday, being overwhelmed by the arrival of the beauteous Koran and by A.'s long letter to L. Thank A. for me. She mustn't insist on protocolian rigour with regard to an answer or a note of thanks from me, but remember the venerable age of her parents to allow them leeway. I am just as grateful for the charming volume, and if I were an ardent churchgoer I should carry it Sunday morning to the tabernacle as if it were a beautifully bound book of Common Prayer. Yesterday we lunched at John Morse's, all of us, and indeed dined there, too. I painfully hobbled there and back. M. Storey

[1] In this letter of April 17, 1928, which appears to be the last that Mr. Perry ever wrote, his physical weakness is apparent in his handwriting, and his characteristic determination to conceal his feelings is no less apparent in his language.

To Joseph C. Grew

wants me to go to Lincoln for a visit next week, but there are so many impediments, in the way of clothes, letters and papers, that I shall probably stay where I am. I was amused by the letter of the Wisconsin boy who asked you for the Ghazi's photograph and signature, etc. Why, you understand of course that it is just for such things that you are where you are. It is your first duty to comply with the demands of your masters, the great American people. The first duty of the President is to sign photographs of himself with one band of idiotic visitors after another. I don't see why we have not the right to insist that you introduce baseball and that the first game shall be opened by the Ghazi, who, like C. C., shall throw a ball somewhere. If you were a hustler, my hints would not be necessary, but you are lamentably out of touch with us home folks. You are too fond of white spats, we prefer the rough stockings of our baseball players. Get to work, hustle a bit! Aristocratic seclusion is a banished 18th century dream. Be a mixer!—There you see me in my solitary corner growling my impotent maledictions on a deaf world. Meanwhile, however, read *Cavour* by Paléologue (Plon, '26, 15 fr.). It's a charming book; my only fear is that you know it already. I have a feeling that you have told me so, but I can't look it up. Farewell, Love from us all to you all. Your grouchy father-in-law, T. S. Perry.

APPENDIX

As this volume was designed and arranged specifically as one of selections from the letters of Mr. Perry, the inclusion of any considerable number of those from his many distinguished friends and contemporaries would be rather out of place, and would involve a problem of selection that would have no particular beginning or end. But a few, which may not be regarded as devoid of a special interest, are printed here as a brief appendix.

This letter from John Addington Symonds, the first of many, is significant as an illustration of Mr. Perry's unconscious power of extracting familiarity and confidence from a total stranger. The deleted portion refers to nothing more mysterious than tuberculosis, which perhaps is always mysterious enough:

Am Hof,
Davos Platz,
Switzerland.
July 15, 1883.

My dear Sir:

Your letter which came to me today, was long indeed, but by no means too long for my taste. Only Americans, I think, have this amiable way of writing in a perfectly frank and friendly style to strangers. It is a way which always wins me, and is, besides, the only way of putting the friendship of two people who may never meet, upon an easy basis.

I have already received Mr. [George] Pellew's essay [on Jane Austen] which I read through the other night with great interest. There is considerable literary promise in its fresh and unaffected style. He, at any rate, one sees, does not intend to be an imitator of Pater's or Swinburne's affectations. Please thank him for the pleasure his essay gave me.

Appendix

You cannot imagine how I envy you that Boston Library! Imagine my conditions. Every book I use, has to be bought and sent from a great distance. Carriage-expenses added to the cost of the books render it a ruinous indulgence to study in Davos with any completeness. And thus, among my many renouncements, one of the hardest to bear is that of thoroughness in literary work. Critics sneer at me for a superficial treatment of some minor department of my subject, unaware that it is less my industry or erudition than my purse on which the blame should be laid.

I should very much like to have any suggestions from you as to points in modern literature. You hint that you might be disposed to send me some. In your investigations of the pre-Renaissance literature, have you studied the Latin poetry of the wandering students—*Carmina Burana* and so forth? I think they would repay a more searching and at the same time sympathetic study than has yet been given them. A tiny volume (*Carmina Vagorum, Teubner*) is a pleasant pocket companion. But I rather fancy that odd girl, Violet Paget, or Vernon Lee as she calls herself in print, is on the subject. I once talked to her about them; and she pitchforks immediately the slightest hint into the robust and original but rather hasty and coarsely grinding mill of her brain.

What a difference there is between your house and mine. Mine is a solid square stone building, with high pitched roof and wooden galleries, standing on a bare bleak wind-swept meadow. There is no vegetation in the valley but grass, pines and larches. It is too cold for corn and fruit trees. Even the rowans I planted round my terrace, have died. In England we had an old grey mansion with a garden full of flowers and fruit trees—greenhouses, graperies, and all the comfortable cosy snugness of green lawns and immemorial elms enclosing jewelled spots of brightness. My wife here is reduced to carnations upon window sills and the geraniums in pots which cotters cultivate, yet I think we love these anxiously tended plants as much as the myriad blooms our gardens used to raise. Also for a month in the year, from the first week in June to the first week in July, the Alpine meadows yield abundance of delicate wild flowers.

If Mr. [Henry] James is with you, will you tell him from me that I know myself in his debt for the most charming bit of writing upon Venice in existence—doubly precious through his corrections. At least I presume that I am right in thinking this. At first I hesitated to write and thank him, not feeling quite sure that he had paid me this distinguished honour. And then when I had made my mind up that I might assume the number of the *Century* to be his gift, I saw his father's death and did not venture to intrude upon him with such a trifle as my thanks.

The MS. of my new book on Eliz: Dr: Lit: is still lying on my study table—ready since last April for the press. But I have had a sharp attack of illness. . . . Deeper than ever plummet sounded I lie inactive.

Appendix

. . . Had I realized the situation, as I realize it now, plain morality would have made me embrace celibacy. My life would probably have been shortened; but one root of mischief in our social system would have been sterilized.

Believe me very faithfully yours,
JOHN ADDINGTON SYMONDS.

Mr. Perry was the first critic, I believe, to call the attention of the American public to the Fitzgerald version of Omar Khayyam—an appreciation that resulted, incidentally, in his unexpected possession of several rare volumes, including a first and second edition of the *Rubaiyat*.

Little Grange, Woodbridge,
Suffolk.
Nov. 23, '75.

Dear Sir:

Mr. Quaritch duly forwarded me your Note. About Omar, I mean. I am sure I ought to be grateful to America for the favour she has shown my old Omar, and to yourself for doing what you have done for me, and now taking the trouble to ask for more of my handy work. That consists chiefly of things taken—I must not say, translated—from foreign sources; and printed partly to give to Friends, and partly because (as I suppose is the case with others) I can only ${\text{alter for} \atop \text{do}}$ my best when Reflected in Type.

So I had some 100 Copies of some of these printed; and, though I have not 100 Friends, I find I am come near an end. As you have taken the trouble to write about them all across the Atlantic, I am glad to be able to send you—perhaps more than you will care to read; none, I feel sure, that you will take Interest in as in Omar. For his *Subject* must interest all us poor Mortal men, right or wrong.

However, I send you another Persian, by way of antidote to him; two Calderon Plays; and Aeschylus' Agamemnon, which I think well of, so far as the Conduct and Dialogue of the Play is concerned.

So now you have drawn on your head more than you bargained for. But there is the Atlantic between us, and you need not read more than you like; nor say anything more about them in reply than that you have received them (I suppose in about some three weeks from this Date).

From your's very truly,
EDWARD FITZGERALD.

Appendix

This note from Tourguéneff is interesting because Tourguéneff wrote it, in English, and because it shows us how he spelt his name:

Thomas S. Perry, Esq.,
   to the care of H. O. Houghton & Co.,
219 Washington Street,
Boston, U. S. A.

                              50, Rue de Donau,
                              Paris.
                              Friday, Oct. 30th, '74.

Sir:
    I have to offer you my warmest thanks for the very flattering article you wrote on my novels in the May No. of the "Atlantic Monthly."—You will excuse the tardiness of my acknowledging it, when you shall know that I have only just read it on my return to France from a voyage to Russia.
    I feel a great sympathy and admiration for your native land and cannot but be very sensible to the judgment of a sagacious and enlightened mind coming from it.

                Believe me, Sir,
                      Yours very truly,
                          IVAN TOURGUÉNEFF.

In spite of Mr. Perry's disapproval of President Wilson, and his friendly relations with Mr. Lodge (which, for political reasons only, were occasionally somewhat strained) he was always an advocate of the League of Nations. These two letters from Mr. Lodge to a friend who did not always agree with him are not uninteresting:

                UNITED STATES SENATE
                              October 14, 1918.

My dear Tom:
    Thank you for your kind note of the 12th, as always helpful and encouraging. The crisis is serious and the President's note of inquiry to the German government meant the opening of discussions. If we get into negotiations with Germany the war is lost, so far as the purposes which alone justify it go. I think it is obvious the country is rising against it, and if it does he will come down or go up, which ever you

Appendix

choose to call it; but I hope and believe that he has created an incurable distrust of his purposes in the mind of the people and that it will show at the polls.

It is most important to get the House and Senate, if we can, out of their present subservient condition and make certain that they at least will stand across the path of any negotiated peace.

Sincerely yours,

H. C. LODGE.

Thomas S. Perry, Esq.,
Hancock, N. H.

UNITED STATES SENATE

September 4, 1919.

Personal.
My dear Tom:

Your letter of the 31st is a real help and encouragement and gives me the greatest pleasure. I like to know you read my speech with interest and approve it and I value particularly what you are good enough to say about its style, for I know that you are a judge of style.

The League as it stands is too dangerous to be accepted, and it can only be saved by efficient reservations. I do not think we shall give much comfort to Germany, for nobody seems desirous of interfering with the terms imposed upon her.

I also like to feel that you and I agree about Mr. Wilson—a very sinister figure in my judgment.

With best regards and thanks,
Ever yours,

H. C. LODGE.

Thomas S. Perry, Esq.,
Hancock, N. H.

Will you give my best regards to your wife and recall to her that I am (in Japanese form) her "profoundly bowing" kinsman.